LESSONS
FOR LIFE
BASED ON THE
LIVES OF
ABRAHAM,
ISAAC,
JACOB
AND
JOSEPH

LESSONS FOR LIFE BASED ON THE LIVES OF ABRAHAM, ISAAC, JACOB AND JOSEPH

PETER ELWOOD

To order additional copies of this book, contact:
Xlibris
800-056-3182
www.Xlibrispublishing.co.uk
Orders@Xlibrispublishing.co.uk
793958

CONTENTS

PREFACE

In the 1970s and 1980s my wife and I were privileged, together with a group of friends: John and Sally, Dennis and Freda, Dave, Richard and Gill, to lead a series of intensive Bible studies with a changing group of undergraduate students each Sunday evening during university term. In preparation for a study we would meet one evening during the week to discuss the passage of Scripture proposed for the following Sunday, and we would share together what we had each learnt from commentaries and other sources. On Sundays, one of us would present the passage for perhaps an hour, and after coffee and biscuits we would have 40 minutes or more open discussion.

Those were life-changing evenings for me. I developed a deep respect for Scripture, a longing to live it out and a desire to share it.

The studies came to an end smoothly and happily, when John and Sally moved to Oxford. This prompted Margaret and me to leave a comfortable down-town church in Cardiff and offer to throw our lot in with a small struggling Baptist church in one of the Welsh valley towns. I offered to take a lead in Bible teaching within the church, and Margaret became involved in 'Time Off', a group for older women, and in a number of other community-based initiatives. After a few months I was invited to accept leadership of the church as a lay, untrained Baptist pastor. After much thought and prayer I accepted…. and so commenced the happiest period of my married life and the busiest period for both of us!

Fourteen years later the church moved to larger premises, led by a gifted local lad with reference to whom I often said: 'I lectured the church, Wayne communicates to the people'!

For each service in the church I typed out an A4 'essay' on the Bible passage which had been preached, and at the end of the service I stood at the door, said Farewell to each person and gave each of them a copy of my essay. In this way I hoped that I might increase both the respect for Scripture throughout the church and perhaps reinforce the memory of each passage presented in the sermon.

When Margaret and I resigned from leadership of the church I rewrote a series of twenty-eight sermons I had given in the church. I had these printed and bound together into a booklet and I gave a copy as a farewell gift to every person who attended the church. These essays have been further edited and are now published under the title: 'A Medical Scientist Examines the Life of Jesus'.

The present volume is based on another series of sermons I had given in the church. These too have been edited and rewritten as a series of essays, under the title:

'Lessons for Life, Based on the Lives of Abraham, Isaac, Jacob and Joseph'.

Peter Elwood,
March 2019

1

GET OUT AND START AGAIN

The call of Abraham
Genesis 11-13 NIV

The writer of Genesis has just described how men decide to fortify themselves and make a name for themselves - all in opposition to God (chapter 11). The name they made has indeed endured - Babel, a Hebrew word, and now our word for confusion! The chapter ends with one man who responded to God, and whose name is truly great. Note the contrast: men, with grandiose projects, jealous of their identity and determined to control their fortunes. On the other hand: one man responding to the call of God and through him God working out His eternal purposes.

Abraham was called by God to leave Ur. Ur means 'light' and may well have been a centre of fire worship. God however does not say 'Go!' to a man. He is always with us and so He says 'Come' (Acts 7.3). Only a response to a true call from God will be sustained. On the other hand, Terah, Abraham's father-in-law, lost the will to persist and so he stayed half-way, at Haran. Abraham however honoured his family commitments, and he remained with Terah until he died (11.31,32) and only then proceeded. Paul later reminded Timothy in rather stark language of the importance of family responsibilities: 'if a man care not for his own, he has denied the faith and is worse than an infidel' (1 Timothy 5.8) NIV.

Notice that the call of God was into blessing (12.2,3). The call of God is seldom negative: 'Quit what you are doing'. Rather His call is positive: 'Come into a new service and into further blessing'. It is worrying when someone who is inactive claims that he is waiting for God to show him what he should do. The fields are white ...get on, man, and do something! God will guide you in your activity for Him. As it has often been pointed out: It is impossible to steer a stationary vehicle! And as Abraham journeyed, he worshipped God. He 'pitched his tent', but he built an altar (12.8). The only relics he left, were to God.

And there was a famine in the land (12.10). What an anti-climax! Abraham had trusted God and had left his home in Ur, and now it all goes wrong! Famine - and in the land promised to him! But God was with him. So he went down into Egypt. Nothing wrong in that - good common sense, as there was food there. But on the way Abraham made a deceitful arrangement with Sarah. They agreed to deny their marriage (12.11-13). As a result things went well - very well indeed in material terms (12.16). But the deceit was discovered and Pharoah threw Abraham out (12.20). What a witness! What a humiliation for a man of God.

Abraham left Egypt a wealthy man (13.2). However he had the right priorities. He returned to Bethel, 'House of God' and called on the Lord there (13.3,4). This was highly significant, because as the writer notes, it had been at Bethel that he had first worshipped God. After the deceit in Egypt, after his humiliation there, he was anxious that his relationship with God was restored. So with us. After failure, we need, by a definite act of confession and submission, to re-establish the Lordship of Christ in our lives.

Throughout these early chapters, there is a most instructive contrast between Abraham and Lot, Abraham's nephew. The stories of the two men are intertwined. Three times Lot is stated to have been a righteous man - but he seems to have made little of it all! Presumably he had had the same call as Abraham as they had left Ur together; they had both had the same experiences of God on the journey, and Lot had probably helped build the altar at Bethel together. Both of them however seem to have been materialists, building up wealth in terms of huge herds of sheep and cattle. Yet while Abraham later sorted out the conflict between his desire for wealth and the call of God, Lot did not. While Abraham seems to have entered into an ever-deepening relationship with God, Lot was drawn away from God and he ended up in a desperate situation in Sodom. We will see all this as the story unfolds. Undoubtedly it is all recorded as a most serious warning to us to get our priorities right. Scripture never condemns wealth, but it warns that a love of money is a root of all kinds of evil, and people who want to get rich fall into temptations and a snare, with many foolish and hurtful desires (1 Timothy 6.9,10) NIV.

Geographers have suggested that the deserts of the Middle East and elsewhere have been caused by overgrazing. Abraham and Lot started it all by amassing herds which the land could not bear (13.5,6). Quarrels broke out and so they agreed to separate. Even though God had promised all the land to him, Abraham is generous, and he gave Lot the choice: 'You go one way and I will go the other' (13.9). There is a most interesting contrast in the way that the two men acted. Lot 'lifted up his eyes' ....and selfishly chose the best land, regardless of the fact that it was adjacent to Sodom, a notorious centre of evil (13.12,13). Abraham however, was told by God to 'lift up his eyes'! He had already been promised the land, and so it had been an act of trust in God on his part to have allowed Lot to make the choice. And immediately after the departure of Lot, Abraham is given reassurance by God, and the promises of blessing are repeated (13.14-17).

So the patterns of their lives begin to develop: Lot moving gradually closer to Sodom, and eventually living in it, while Abraham was building altars to God (13.18) NIV.

2

PEOPLE, THINGS
AND GOD - GET
THEM SORTED!

Abraham, Lot and Melchisidec
Genesis 14 NIV

*A mysterious figure appears in this chapter: Melchisidec. Little is known
about him. Later, the Bible makes two statements about him which
indicate his importance: Melchisidec was 'made like unto the Son of
God' (Hebrews 7.3) and Christ is a priest 'after the order of Melchisidec'
(Hebrews 5.10). This all suggests that something special about the
Lord Jesus Christ can be learnt from study of this man Melchisidec.*

Chapter 13 has left Lot making his home in the lush pastures near the
city of Sodom (12), while Abraham, still in the land to which God had
called him, was building yet another altar to his God (18).

Chapter 14 is full of drama! Various 'kings', or desert sheiks are
mentioned. References to many of these have been found in other
ancient writings. While one might wish for more details of the events
recorded, the focus of the narrative is clearly on the faith of one man, and
the rivalries and battles between these desert sheiks are incidental to the
eternal purposes of God. The relevance of the squabbles becomes clear
in verse 11: Lot is taken prisoner. Notice however that Lot is now said
to be living in Sodom, and note also the emphasis given by the ordering

of things listed in verses 11 and 12: 'goods ...food ...possessions'. Lot seems to now be a gross, blatant materialist!

Abraham learns of the plight of Lot, and in a very short passage the loyalty of Abraham, his skill in battle and his rescue of Lot is told. Again however, notice the emphasis upon 'goods ...possessions' and how the writer adds, almost as an afterthought, that in addition to the goods, women were also rescued (16)!

Abraham returns from the rescue, with his 318 armed men, Lot, and a rabble of people all laden with goods. And suddenly, a mysterious figure, Melchisidec, meets them (18). Picture the scene: Abraham weary from battle, irritated no doubt by the cries of the rabble, and this man Melchisidec interrupts him in order to give him a blessing! Put yourself in the place of Ab. 'What good is that prayer, Melc.? What are you on about? Tell me how to cope with this lot. Give us some help man, some shelter and don't go on about blessings. There is a time and a place....'.

The names given by men to God are of immense interest, and the first use of each of these is usually in some situation where the aspect of the character of God indicated by the name, is of special relevance to those who use it first. So it is here. Melchisidec uses two names for God which are new, and which indicated aspects of God which were shortly to become of crucial relevance to Abraham.

But first, look briefly at the rest of the chapter. Verse 21 states that the King of Sodom, an evil and perverted materialist, hears about Abraham's victory, and he sets out to meet him. So Sodom and Abraham are travelling towards each other - and suddenly Melchisidec interposes himself between them. An evil pervert and a godly pilgrim are about to meet! A materialist, and a man seeking 'a heavenly city'! This will be no ordinary meeting. And Melchisidec, priest of the most high God ('who was made like unto the Son of God') interposes himself and prepares Abraham for the encounter - just as our High Priest does with us!

The names of God which are used by Melchisidec are of crucial relevance to the situation. Abraham is told that God is 'the most high' (El Elyon) and He is the 'Possessor of all things' ('Creator' in many translations - the difference matters little). However little the relevance of this bit of theology may have seemed to Abraham at the time of his meeting with Melchisidec, it became the answer to his dilemma the next day when he met Sodom. So it is with our Great High Priest. He would prepare us **beforehand** for crises to come. Furthermore, the lessons of today, however remote they may seem from the problems of Monday morning, may be no less than His answer for those very problems. Watch carefully as the story develops.

Abraham the pilgrim, meets Sodom, the pervert, in verse 21. 'Ab., you're something of a materialist. You have recovered all these goods - and well you deserve them. You keep them and I'll take the people - and don't ask what I'll do with them!' But Abraham said: I have raised my hand to El Elyon, the Most High, the Possessor, the Creator of all things': I'm not answerable to you, Sodom, and neither you nor I have any rights over these things, or these folk. The most High God created them all, and it is to Him alone that we are answerable. I'll not touch your dirty deal!

Watch it Ab! Sodom isn't a man to be spurned. Like most men of the world, we're all in it together and if I offer to scratch your back don't you dare kick me in the teeth! But God reassured Abraham in a vision that night: .... don't worry about Sodom, 'I am your Shield', and don't have any second thoughts about having lost out on a good deal: 'I am you very great reward' (15.1).

This meeting of Abraham and Melchisidec clearly had a great effect on Abraham, and a change in his whole attitude and in the priorities, he set in his life appear to have changed from that point on. But before we leave the incident, we should return to the comments made by the writer to the Hebrews about the similarities between Jesus and Melchisidec. Jesus claimed to be the way, the truth and the life. He Himself went on to explain how He is the way to God, and the rest of the New Testament expounds the concept of Him as the life. Relatively little is said directly however about Him being the truth, though Paul does state that 'the truth is in Jesus' (Ephesians 4.21). Does this incident with Melchisidec help us put flesh onto this statement? Abraham, about to be confronted by Sodom, learns truths about the character and the nature of God - truths which are of basic relevance to his situation the next day, when he meets Sodom. Does this indicate that the truths that will help us, when facing difficulties and temptations, have been displayed in human terms and in human situations by Jesus, the Son of God - and so, Christ is a priest for us 'after the order of Melchisidec' (Hebrews 5.10) NIV.

3

A BASIC AGREEMENT

Abraham alone with God
Genesis 15 NIV

*In obeying God and by living out what he is learning about God,
Abraham is being drawn into an ever deepening relationship with God.
On the basis of the trust he has demonstrated, God now declares Abram
to be righteous (15.6). Inspired commentaries on this verse are in Romans
4.3, Galatians 3.6 and James 2.23. It is the first, clear statement in
Scripture of the basis upon which God counts a man acceptable.*

The crisis with Sodom over, Abraham's desire focuses upon a son
(15.2,3). What is the point of being given lands if he has no heir to
inherit? God could easily have granted the wish of Abraham there
and then. Why did He not? Why were Abraham and Sarah kept in
suspense during six chapters, covering about twenty-five years? Was it
because of the basic human principle that men seldom learn through
easy solutions, most of us learn best through situations of uncertainly
and difficulty - and through failure! As one writer has put it: God is
concerned with character rather than comfort.

So God kept Abraham in a state of tension and uncertainty. One
wonders if Abraham was basically somewhat unbalanced: early in his
relationship with God he had had to sort out his evaluation of people
and things, and later, when he did have a son, God had to take him
through a dreadful test by ordering him to give back his son (Ch.22).

Was it in this last, as he sorted out his evaluation of his son and of God that he reached the final true balance of values?

Notice the sequence in the record of the dialogue between Abraham and God: 'Lord, I am childless' ...'You will have a son and your descendants will be uncountable' ...'Lord how can I be certain of all this?' (15.8). And then occurs the statement: Abraham believed God and God counted it to him as righteousness.

A meaningful and a helpful definition of faith is: a positive response to evidence. Faith is not a blind leap in the dark. That is simple gullibility. God gives us evidence and we trust him on the basis of evidence. The response of trust then takes us beyond the evidence in the immediate situation, into situations within which we may have no direct evidence. So it is in salvation, and so it is in the growth of faith in the believer. After all, God made us to respond within human relationships in this manner, so why should our relationship with Him be of a different kind. A man marries a girl 'in faith', but not in blind faith. He has no direct knowledge as to how his fiancée will cope later with their children, how she will behave as he ages, how she will respond during his terminal illness. Presumably however, the girl will have given him evidence as to her dependability and faithfulness in lesser crises. And so, in response to limited evidence, he launches into a new relationship with the girl - in faith!

And so, on the basis of evidence which had already been given, Abraham believed God (15.6). Yet in 15.8 he asks 'How can I believe?' Lord, I do trust You, but I have no basis upon which to believe Your promise regarding this new situation. In other words: 'Lord I believe, help my unbelief?' And so God gave Him further evidence, and on the basis of that evidence of God's dependability, Abraham waits, in faith, for twenty-five years. So it is with us: if we take our doubts to Him, He will give us further evidence, and as we receive that further evidence, so our trust deepens.

Abraham illustrates all this. Having worked out his trust in God as Creator and Possessor in his interview with Sodom, his trust with respect to the promise of a son now stretches his faith, and so God graciously gave him further evidence in terms of a covenant, or an explicit commitment.

Even today, the making of a covenant, such as a marriage, or a business partnership, is no light thing. Statements and promises are made and signed before witnesses. In Abraham's day the making of a covenant was no less complex and there was certain ceremonial to be followed. The men who wished to enter into a covenant would kill an animal and cut it in pieces. This gave the ancient Hebrews their word for a covenant, namely: to 'cut' a covenant. The men would repeat the words of the agreement and then walk between the pieces of the animal saying words such as 'The Lord do so to me and more also if I keep not the words of this covenant' (see Jeremiah 34.18-19) NIV.

All this is enacted in the covenant God made with Abraham, as recorded in the second half of Genesis 15. There is however one important difference. Covenants between men were made as between equals, and both took an active part in the ceremonial. God however is no man's equal. He alone sets the terms of the agreement and the covenant is offered to man freely, to accept in faith. All the action is therefore by God, while Abraham slept and played no active part in the ceremony. Thus while men can enter freely into all the benefits of a covenant which is made by God, yet at the same time they come under the obligations of the covenant. God alone stated the benefits of the covenant (15.13-21), but He then commanded Abraham to keep the obligations of the covenant: 'Walk before Me and be thou perfect' (17.1).

Later, when the descendants of Abraham had multiplied and were about to enter the land which had been promised to Abraham, God brought Israel into a covenant relationship with Himself. Exodus 24 describes how the terms of the covenant were read, animals were sacrificed, blood was sprinkled, and a covenant meal was held. The Israelites of course failed to keep their responsibilities under the covenant and so that covenant was broken (Exodus 32) and had to be re-established by Moses on behalf of the people (Exodus 34).

Later, the covenant with Israel was broken so often that Israel became 'Lo Ami': 'Not My people', and God warned them that they would be judged for their disobedience. At the same time, God, through Jeremiah, stated that the covenant with Israel would be replaced (Jeremiah 31.31-33). And in due course, Jesus died, and in His blood 'A New Covenant' was established. The writer to the Hebrews says much about this, and in one passage he seems to have in mind a will, or a last testament (Hebrews 9.15). A will is of course a covenant, and as the writer of Hebrews states, a will is of no force until the testator dies. Thus, the New Covenant had to be established by the death of Jesus. As with the covenant with Abraham, this new covenant is all of God, and He has stated the four benefits (these are listed in Hebrews 8.10-12 and 10.16,17). And again there are obligations, and so Scripture urges us, that before we take the symbols of the New Covenant, the bread and the wine, that we examine ourselves as to how we have been keeping the obligations of the covenant (1 Corinthians 11.28). The charge to Abraham is timeless: 'Walk before Me and be thou perfect' (17.1).

[handwritten margin note: New Covenant not replaced]

4

A TRIANGLE OF RELATIONSHIPS!

Abraham, Sarah and Hagar
Genesis 16 NIV

Abraham had learnt many lessons and his walk was bringing him closer and closer to God. Nevertheless, he had an overwhelming desire for a son and this longing for an heir coloured much of his thinking. Despite repeated assurances by God, the doubts of Abraham seem to have overcome his trust in God.

Abraham was probably put under some pressure by his wife. She was well past the age of child bearing and so she persuaded Abraham to have relations with her maid. The presence of Hagar may well have stemmed from the episode in Egypt, when Abraham had denied his wife. Here again, in effect, Abraham denies his wife, with even worse results this time.

When Hagar becomes pregnant Sarah found her presence unacceptable and the inevitable triangle resulted. Their bad interrelationships led to scandalous behaviour: Hagar's pregnancy made her arrogant (16.4), Sarah told Abraham it was all his fault (5) and Abraham washed his hands of the whole sorry business (6). The tranquillity of the home of Sarah and Abraham was shattered, and it was probably never the same again. And so it always is. Human relationships are exceedingly vulnerable and any betrayal of trust, anything less that total and enduring commitment will inevitably lead to unhappiness, distrust and worse. Of all relationships, marriage is the most vulnerable, though when developed aright, no relationship has such potential for happiness and fulfilment.

Abraham had taken things into his own hands. Instead of trusting God, he had been guided by Sarah. No excuse for Abraham is made in Scripture though the contrast between Ishmael and Isaac is drawn out later in Galatians 4. Paul there argues that Ishmael, a child generated by the will of man, and Isaac, a son born of the promise of God, are allegories of the natural and the spiritual; the earthly and the heavenly; that which is below and that which is from above; the slave and the free (Galatians 4.22-31). This passage by Paul goes further and makes reference to the old covenant established with Israel at Mount Sinai, standing for works, and the new covenant established by Jesus Christ at Jerusalem, standing for faith (24-26).

Abraham tries to wash his hands of the whole mess he has created by impregnating Hagar, but the evil that men do, lives on. Sarah behaves so badly that Hagar flees into the desert and nearly perishes. 'The Angel of the Lord' came to her and told her to return to Hagar and Abraham. The name given later to her child (Ishmael: God shall hear) indicates His care - even for the outcast.

Abraham treated Ishmael well, though his feelings seem to have been somewhat mixed. Despite the repeated promises by God, and despite His covenant, Abraham seems to have had gnawing doubts about the likelihood of Sarah ever bearing a child. So, later, when the promise was repeated thirteen years after the birth of Ishmael, Abraham laughed, and pleaded: 'If only Ishmael might live under your blessing' (17.18). In answer, God states that Ishmael would indeed be blessed and would become a great nation, but His covenant of special blessing will apply to his son by Sarah and his descendants by her (17.18-20). Despite all this, Abraham is distressed when tension develops between his two sons, Ishmael and Isaac, and Ishmael and his mother have to leave (21.11-14) NIV.

Despite the fact that Ishmael was brought up in a godly home and despite the prayers of Abraham for him, Ishmael is said to have been a wild man (in the Hebrew this is literally: 'a wild ass of a man'), and it was prophesied that he would be against every man and every man against him '...he will live in hostility towards all his brothers' (16.12). This last phrase has certainly been true, but so also has been an alternative translation of the phrase: 'he will live amongst his brothers'. The Arabs have lived amongst the Jews in a state of constant enmity ever since.

Abraham sinned in having relationships with Hagar, outside marriage. Undoubtedly, he repented and his relationship with God was clearly restored. Forgiveness however is not a simple matter. Although a sin may be forgiven, although the guilt can be removed and the punishment born vicariously by Jesus on the cross, yet the consequences in terms of wrong to our fellow men, remains. Despite the repentance of Abraham for his sin against God's moral law, Ismael lived on, and Abraham and others had to handle the consequences. In exactly the same way, David repented for the sin of his adultery with Bathsheba and his murder of Uriah, her husband, and he was told: 'The Lord has put away your sin'. But he was told the consequences: 'the child will surely die' (2 Samuel 12.13,14). In his own commentary on this shameful incident (Psalm 51), David states that his sin has been against God, and this has been forgiven, but the wrong was against Bathsheba, and she and he were bereaved by the loss of the child.

Meanwhile, Abraham moves ever closer to God. The beginning of Chapter 17 marks a high point in their relationship. Men who entered into a covenant relationship sometimes took new names, and so here Abram (perhaps meaning 'High father') becomes Abraham ('Father of nations'). God too, took a new name: El Shaddai, God Almighty, or, God who is sufficient, a most important name, often associated later with the covenant. Abraham had left Ur and staked all on the promises of God. Was he rash? Not at all! God is the 'All sufficient' for every need of Abraham in this world and in the next.

5

A MAN WITH A MUCK RAKE!

Abraham and Lot
Genesis 19 NIV

*In Pilgrim's Progress Bunyan showed Christiana a tableau of a man with
a muck-rake in his hand. The man kept endlessly raking over a pile of
wood, hay and stubble, looking for something, anything of value. Above
his head was an angel holding out a crown, but the man was so intent on
raking the muck that he never noticed.*
Abraham had grasped the crown. Lot held onto the muck-rake!

There are few more sharp contrasts in these stories that that between
Abraham and Lot. They had had the same beginnings and the same
opportunities. Both had left Ur in response to a call of God. Both had
had further experiences of God and presumably both had built altars
along the way. Both had had faith in God and both were declared
righteous by God.

But here the similarities end. Both had been blessed by God and both
had become wealthy, but while Abraham had sorted out his evaluation
of people, of wealth, and his evaluation of his relationship with God,
Lot had gradually moved away from God into the world - in the worst
meaning of this word. Abraham sought God and was obedient. Success
led Lot away from God and he came to set his heart on material things.

While Abraham became 'the friend of God', Lot became more and more involved in the affairs of a most evil city.

At the start of the account in Genesis, Lot and Abraham had had to separate because of their huge flocks (13.7-9). Abraham had given Lot the choice, and he had decided to settle in the lush pasturage of the plain, even though the neighbouring town was noted for its perversions. Shortly after he had settled there, desert sheiks had swooped on Sodom and taken the people, including Lot. Abraham, who is beginning to sort out 'people and things' rescued Lot and on the return journey to Sodom, Melchisidec had met them. Although Lot must have heard the teaching by Melchisidec, it seems to have had no effect on him and at the next mention of Lot, he is back in Sodom.

Chapter 18 records a remarkable episode in the life of Abraham, when he dined and conversed with Jesus in pre-incarnate form. Perhaps this is the incident referred to by Jesus when He said, as recorded in John 8.56: 'Abraham rejoiced to see My day, and he saw it and was glad'. The incident may also lie behind the statement in Hebrews 13.2: 'Entertain strangers, for thereby some have entertained angels'. How our dining rooms would be transformed if we acted like Abraham! Of course these had been no ordinary visitors, and two, who were angelic, went on into Sodom and were involved in its destruction. Abraham however, is said to have 'stood before the Lord' and to have pleaded for the lives of the men of Sodom (23-33). In this, Abraham demonstrated first, the depth of his relationship with God, and second, the extent to which he had sorted out 'people and things'. But the key to Abraham's part in this event is indicated in verses 17-19. The Lord asked: 'Can I hide from Abraham what things I am about to do'. Here is the basis of true friendship - communication! It is to the extent that we share our thoughts and our intentions that we truly make friends of our partner, members of our family and others. Jesus said as much to His disciples: ' Now I shall not call you servants, for the servant knoweth not, what his lord shall do; but I have called you friends, for all things whatever I heard of my Father, I have made known to you' (John 15.15) NIV.

As it was with Abraham, as it was with the disciples, so it is with us - communication is the basis of true friendship.

Meanwhile Lot has become involved in the affairs of Sodom and he is now 'sitting in the gate'. The gate of an ancient city was not just a hole in the wall, it was a complex structure with various rooms within which the administration of the city took place. Lot had therefore become deeply involved in the affairs of Sodom.

While Abraham was discussing the purposes of God, the two angels went to Lot. He received them and offered them hospitality. The two men declined, but Lot knew the men of Sodom and so he insisted on giving them shelter for the night (19.3). During the night a foul situation developed. A crowd of perverts gathered and clamoured for the guests of Lot (4,5). To appease them, Lot made an offer so ghastly that it doesn't bear repeating (see verse 8). The angels smote the perverts with blindness, and they urged Lot and his family to leave the city and flee. The witness of Lot had however lost all credibility and his sons in law thought he was joking (14)! The affairs of the city had developed such a hold on Lot that he had to be dragged out of the city (16). Even then, he pleads to be allowed to stay in a neighbouring city (20).

The end of Lot is sordid beyond. He became a caveman (30) and his two daughters committed incest with him (31-38). They gave birth to the progenitors of two of the most aggressive tribes, Moab and Amon.

And all Lot had done at the start was to 'pitch his tent towards Sodom'. But one compromise had led to another - downwards! While Abraham became the friend of God, Lot ended up with the muck rake grasped firmly in his hand.

6

TRUTHS AND HALF-TRUTHS

Abraham and a local official
Genesis 20-21 NIV

Abraham has had the most incredible experience (Ch.18). He has dined with the Lord incarnate, he has learned something of His purposes, he had interceded for others and he had seen judgement fall on Sodom. Despite all this, he behaves dishonourably and lapses into petty dishonesty and half-truths.

Abraham moved north and came to two cities. He surmised that the people were not God fearing and he feared for his life and for the life of Sarah. He told the local official, Abimelech, that Sarah was his sister and he allowed Abimelech to take her into his harem. A sorry repeat of the incident in Egypt (12.10-20). Will the man never learn?

That night God gave Abimelech a vision and he learnt the truth about Sarah. He pleaded ignorance and asks: 'Will God slay a righteous nation?' God acknowledged his innocence and told him that Abraham will pray for him! All reminiscent of the earlier episode in Egypt (18).

But the confrontation between Abraham and Abimelec is more dramatic than that which had occurred in the earlier incident with Pharaoh. On that occasion Pharaoh had simply thrown Abraham out. Now, Abimelech rebukes Abraham, and Ab. fumbling with half-truths mutters: 'I thought you were all godless ...I feared you would murder me ...she is my half-sister, ...and, and, and...' worst of all '...it was all because the gods made me wander from my old home' (13). What a way to refer to his call by Almighty God to leave Ur!

The importance of this whole incident lies in the fact that Sarah was about to bear the long-promised son. Between chapter 18, when Sarah was told that she would become pregnant, and the birth of Isaac in chapter 21, one year elapsed. Any infidelity on the part of Sarah could put the parentage of her child in doubt. God had promised that Abraham would be the father and so the fact that Abimelech had not even touched Sarah had to be made public (see verses 6 and 8). Such was the concern of God for the purity of the promised line - the line which of course led to His own beloved Son, Jesus Christ.

Abimelech reappears later in Chapter 21. He has been watching Abraham after their confrontation and he now acknowledges: 'God is with you in all you do' (22). At the same time he does not fully trust Abraham and he asks Abraham to swear that he would not be false again (23). Lies and deception can be confessed and repented of, but consequences remain in terms of a lack of trust, and friendship may never be fully restored after an episode of deception.

In fact, the friendship between Abraham and Abimelech was very soon tested again. Their herdsmen quarrelled over a well. On this occasion Abraham behaved honourable and he made a covenant with Abimelec (literally they 'cut a covenant' in verse 27). Because of this they called the well Beersheba: 'the well of the oath'. The whole incident however has a ring of unease about it and there is no evidence of any lasting friendship between the men. Indeed it is no surprise that later Abimelech quarrelled with Isaac over this same well (26.17-32). The consequences of deceit are far and long reaching indeed!

The chapter ends with Abraham looking back and reviewing the past few incidents: his deception and Abimelech's continuing distrust of him, their recent quarrel and the flimsy agreement they had made. Turning from it all, Abraham looks up, and calling on the name of the Lord he gives God a new name: El Olam, 'the everlasting God'. Men are fickle - above all, Abraham himself - but God is dependable, and He, only He, is everlasting, the same yesterday, today and for ever!

It is interesting that among all these events the birth of Isaac has passed almost unnoticed. There is a quiet confidence in the statement: 'the Lord did for Sarah as He had promised ...at the very time God had promised' (21.1,2). No surprise! The promises of God are utterly dependable. But had the birth been recorded by a human hand alone, there would probably have been a flowery, triumphant description of the event.

Some time later, perhaps at his coming of age, Abraham prepared a feast for Isaac. This made his half-brother, Ishmael, jealous and he mocked Isaac. Abraham couldn't take it. Ishmael was a bad-tempered wild man, and so to ensure the safety of Isaac, Ishmael had to be sent packing with his mother. But Abraham still had a fondness for the lad. He had interceded for him and God had reassured Abraham that he would be blessed and his descendants would become a great nation.

Ishmael and his mother leave home and wander in the desert. Yet God cares even for the outcast, and provides for him (16-20). The translation of this statement (21) that Ishmael became an archer, is perhaps closer to the truth in the Jewish Chumash: 'he became a robber'!

7

GIVE YOUR SON BACK

Abraham and Isaac
Genesis 22 NIV

With help from Melchisidec Abraham has sorted out his evaluation of people and things, now he is challenged on the priority of relationships. His and Sarah's consuming desire for a son has at long last been fulfilled. The friction between Ishmael and Isaac has been settled, painfully but decisively. Abraham is now comforted in his old age as he watches Isaac grow to maturity. As he will have watched Isaac grow, Abraham will have meditated on the promises of God, and on the covenant, all of which focussed on that lad alone, and on how all the nations would be blessed through him.

Suddenly, the tranquillity of old age is shattered by the command: 'Give Me back your son'! The horror must have been heightened by the way God referred to Isaac as 'Your only son, whom you love' (2).

Isaac was to be sacrificed on Mount Moriah (2), the mountain on which the Temple was later built, and the place where, much later, another greatly loved Only Son would die on a cross. Abraham set out early in the morning on the three day journey to Mount Moriah (3), perhaps an indication as to how he had had to steel himself for the task. Verse 5 is notable in indicating the faith of Abraham in the conviction that somehow he and the lad would return. In fact, the divine commentary on this incident in Hebrews states that Abraham's confidence in the promises of God was such that he trusted that God was able to raise his son up from the dead (Hebrews 11.19) NIV.

This statement by Abraham to the men accompanying them, that he and Isaac would worship and then return, is the first use in Scripture of the work 'worship'. Does this indicate the 'worth-ship' Abraham put on God and on His commands? Whatever we make of the word in this particular verse, it is of interest that Scripture uses the word 'worship' for the service of God as well as for the mental and spiritual reverence we express to God. And the first use of the word suggests the importance of 'worship' expressed in obedience and in what a man does for God.

On their way to the place of sacrifice Isaac asked his father an immortal question: 'Where is the lamb for the sacrifice?' Man in every age has asked such a question. 'Where are the grounds for my acceptance by a holy God?' And man in every culture has devised this own answer: the best of the crops, the best of his possessions, his own good works etc. The question remained unanswered for two millenia - until John the Baptist cried: 'Behold the Lamb of God that takes away the sin of the world' (John 1.29).

The answer of Abraham to the question of Isaac (8) has been much debated: 'God will provide Himself a Lamb for the burnt offering' in the AV, or 'God Himself will provide the Lamb' in the NIV. Either way, Abraham seems to have known that no sacrifice from man would atone for sin. God Himself would have to provide the atoning sacrifice. Hence Abraham later called the place 'Jehovah-Jireh' (the Lord will provide). But if the AV rendering of the passage is correct, Abraham may have had some inkling that the sacrifice he was being called upon to make with his son, was prophetic of a far greater offering. And if so, and if Abraham did have some insight into the provision God would make in His Son, then this may again explain the statement by Jesus Himself: 'Abraham rejoiced to see My day; he saw it and was glad' (John 8.56).

What lies behind this mysterious incident? The chapter commences: 'After these things, God tested Abraham.' After what things? The immediately preceding events had been the birth of Isaac and the dismissal of Ishmael and Hagar. There had probably therefore been an increasing focus of attention by Abraham on Isaac, and perhaps this had led to a lessening of communion between Abraham and God. It may therefore have been that God was saying: 'In whom are you trusting, Abraham? In whom do your hopes lie? On what is your heart really set? In what lies 'your exceeding great reward?' (15.2) Take your son Abraham and give him back to Me!'

But God took Abraham through that dreadful experience for another reason, and one that is essential for every Christian to learn. Belief in God is not enough. After all, as James points out: 'The devils believe and tremble' (James 2.19). God demands evidence of belief in terms of obedience. In fact, James is prepared to say that the need for an evidence of faith, in terms of obedience to God, is so great that in one sense Abraham was saved by his works!

All this last is confirmed in the passage in Genesis 22 when it states that the angel of the Lord said to Abraham: 'Don't harm your son ...for now I know that you fear God' (12). This is incredible! Did God not know the state of Abraham's heart before this incident? Of course He did, but He still requires evidence from every believer, in terms of active obedience to His word.

8

THE ETERNAL PERSPECTIVE

Death is not the end
Genesis 23,24 NIV

The story of Abraham draws to a close and
very shortly Isaac takes the stage.
The attitude of a man to eternity shows clearly
in how he handles the death
of a loved one, and in how he approaches
his own passing.

The account of the death of Sarah is sad, but triumphant! Together she and Abraham had left Ur. Together they had made mistakes but through them they had come to an ever increasing experience of God in their lives. Perhaps their 'togetherness' is especially recorded in the name given to the place where she died: Hebron. It means: 'union'. It is not clear however whether this commemorates the union of the couple, or their union with God. Perhaps both!

Christian marriage can be like that. Eternal life was later defined by Jesus as getting to know God and the One whom He sent (John 17.3), and if a couple get to know Him together, reading, praying and discussing the things of God together, encouraging and supporting each other and developing some area of Christian work together, then their home with be in 'Hebron' and their death with be in 'Hebron'.

Few, if any of us, develop our marriage partnership as we should, and yet the potential of a human union 'in Christ' must be infinite. Paul, in Ephesians 5, inter-twines teaching about a man and his wife with teaching about Christ and His church, implying that as a couple work out their marriage, they will learn more about the mystic union between Christ and His church, and His love for it. John points out to us that the evidence we have of God's love, is that He laid down His life for us (1 John 3.16), and so, John continues, we ought to lay down our lives for others. It is perhaps unfortunate that we usually see this phrase as meaning the giving of life in death. In fact, the phrase constitutes a far more realistic challenge: we can 'give our lives' in service to others.

A most instructive incident follows as Abraham bargains for a plot of land for the burial of Sarah. Note the dignity, and the 'eternal perspective' with which Abraham speaks and acts. The natives, the Hittites, refer to him, as 'a prince with God'. Clearly they had been watching him, and it was perhaps his conduct at the time of the death of his wife that specially impressed them. So it is with us. How we behave when death touches someone close to us will show whether or not we really do have an eternal perspective. Then, despite his having lived in Canaan for years, Abraham refers to himself as a 'stranger and pilgrim'.

In this somewhat casual opening to the bargaining process over the plot of land, Abraham betrays his eternal vision. The phrase is taken up elsewhere in Scripture (and also by John Bunyan). In Hebrews 11: Abraham is said to have called himself 'a stranger and pilgrim on earth ...looking forward to the city with foundations, whose architect and builder is God'. Later, Peter wrote to the 'pilgrims and strangers' scattered throughout the Jewish dispersion. In other words, the focus and interest of Abraham, and Sarah, had been on heavenly things and they looked lightly on the things of this world. Alas, although many of us can use phrases like these, most of us are caught up, and even bound to the material world.

And yet, Abraham did want a stake in this world! God had repeatedly promised him the land of Canaan and as yet he owned none of it. As Hebrews comments about the patriarchs: 'They did not receive the things promised, they only saw them and welcomed them from a distance'. All Abraham owned was the cave of Mackpelah, where he buried Sarah - and he had had to purchase it! The great man Abraham, recipient of eternal promises from Almighty God - and all he has to bequeath to his son, is a graveyard! And yet, Abraham's desire to bury Sarah, and later to be buried himself within the promised land indicates their conviction that in some way God would fulfil His promise to them, and therefore their future, even after death, would be linked to the land. As Calvin put it: 'While they themselves were silent, the sepulchre cried aloud that death formed no obstacle to their entering in to the possession of it'.

And so Abraham and Seth go through the eastern courtesies of bargaining. Ephron, the owner of the land, wants to give it to Abraham. Perhaps he is apprehensive about a powerful man like Abraham getting a foothold in his land. Better to give it, and put Abraham under an obligation to him. But Abraham had learnt from Melchisidec not to accept undeserved favours, and so he insists on paying.

After the death of Sarah Abraham fades from the story and the focus moves to Isaac. The death of Abraham is however instructive. He died, the record says, and 'was gathered to his people' (25.8). This can hardly refer simply to the fact that he was buried alongside Sarah, in the cave of Macpelah. The phrase arises rather from a conviction that 'his people' still existed beyond the grave. Of course, this is no surprise. After all, Job, who probably lived well before Abraham, spoke with utter confidence of his Redeemer whom he would see after death 'and not as a stranger' (Job 19.27 AV margin) NIV.

How will we face the end? Will the manner of our passing give evidence of an 'eternal perspective? In speaking prophetically of the death of Peter, Jesus indicated that his confidence in His Lord as he died would be so great that his passing would 'glorify God' (John 21.19) NIV.

9

A CONSISTENT BELIEVER

Holding on and passing on
Genesis 24,26 NIV

Isaac is sometimes dismissed as a somewhat colourless character.
Unlike Abraham, he was no pioneer, no striding out into the unknown,
following the call of God. And yet, and yet...

Isaac should be a tremendous encouragement to us. Few of us are called to be pioneers, or to do some memorable work for God. Very few of us can claim to have had any great vision, or any deep insight into the mind or the work of God. Perhaps therefore we can identify with Isaac more readily than with Abraham. Isaac was a quiet man and no great incident is recorded about him, yet he was deeply convinced and his relationship with God affected his whole attitude and his way of life. A thumb-nail sketch of him could be: 'he held on and he passed on'! That is all most of us are called upon to do! There have to be pioneers, church planters, evangelists, but the strength of the church ultimately lies in the consistent godly lives of 'average' Christians.

The story of the servant of Abraham finding a bride for Isaac (chapter 24) is one of the best love-stories ever written. But it is far more than this and many commentators see in it a picture of the Holy Spirit finding and preparing a bride for Christ. The parallels are beautiful. Rebecca left all and was drawn to a man whom she had never seen, but about whom she had learnt from the servant - just as the Christian is drawn by love to Christ, and the Holy Spirit ministers the things of Christ to us. Because of her union with Isaac, Rebecca became an heir to all the blessings of God and she became involved in the great and eternal purposes of God - just as the Christian becomes a joint-heir with Christ and enters into blessings prepared from before the foundations of the world. Also, the self-effacing way that the servant claims nothing for himself, but exalts his master, reminds us of the Holy Spirit whom Jesus said, takes the things of Christ and makes them known to us (John 16.13) NIV.

Isaac loved Rebecca dearly and their union seems to have been loving and complete. Theirs will have been a godly home and their two boys will have been told repeatedly about God's dealings with Abraham, and about the promises and blessings of God. But one of them couldn't have cared less. Esau was a man of the world and he despised it all (Hebrews12.16). Jacob was different - not very different at first, because he was a cheat and a deceiver, but he did value the things of God and although it took him many years, he did eventually sort himself out and bring his life under the government of God. Two very different boys, though both received the same upbringing and the same godly instruction.

The consistency of Isaac as a believer is however best shown in chapter 26. The chapter starts with disaster. A famine develops and God encourages Isaac to remain where he is ...rest in My promises, and I will be with you (3). But tragedy ensues in another sordid episode of deception. Despite the care and the promises of God, Isaac risks it all, and he jeopardises the sanctity of his wife just to ensure his own safety (7). The deceit is discovered and the men of Gehar show themselves to be highly honourable. They rebuke Isaac for his lies.

The incident of deception left a nasty atmosphere and although it seems to have been forgiven relationships were strained and hostility developed over the ownership of some wells. One dishonourable act can destroy trust and sour relationships thereafter. How important that the Christian is upright in all his dealings especially with unbelievers.

Isaac however had learnt his lesson and he lived quietly and honourably. No more deception, no more lies. The chapter ends with the men of Gehar coming to him and acknowledging that they saw that God was with him. What a change from the rebuke they had given earlier to the commendation they now give: 'We see that the Lord is certainly with you' (28). What a testimony. Would our neighbours ever say that they see that God is with us?

Another, even more telling testimony was later paid to the consistency of Isaac by his own son. Jacob, when in a difficult situation (31.42), Jacob referred to God as 'the fear of my father Isaac'. Jacob of course used the word fear in the sense of One who was regarded with reverence and respect. How will my children refer to God? Will they ever refer to Him as the One their father worshipped and served?

Not that the godly attitude of Isaac was enough for Jacob. Conformity is often the path of least resistance and religious attitudes and practices can easily be passed from father to son. Real convictions are however never second-hand. Every man must find God for himself and enter into his own personal relationship with Him. Paul wrote: 'Let every man be convinced in his own mind' and he went on to warn that one day every knee will bow to Jesus Christ, as Lord. That is: let every man think things through for himself, on his knees, and let him reach his own conviction as to the lordship of Christ, and let him do so with the final judgement in mind!

'If a man would live well, let him fetch his last day and make it his company-keeper' (Bunyan).

10

UNPROMISING BEGINNINGS

Jacob - the home wrecker!
Genesis 25,27 NIV

*The twins, Jacob and Esau, will have had the same background,
and the same godly upbringing. Yet one became a man of the
world, caring nothing for the promises of God and God's covenant
with his family. The story is complex however, because although
the other twin cared deeply for these things, yet he comes over as
a nasty, deceptive, selfish lad, who cheated all around him - his
brother, his father and his uncle. In the end however, Jacob sorted
himself out - or rather God sorted him out, and he came into a deep
relationship with God. His search for God now becomes the theme.*

The difference between Esau and Jacob is shown somewhat starkly at
the end of Chapter 25 (29-34). Esau returned from hunting. He was
famished and he saw Jacob with some porridge. He asked for some of
it and in the original his language was crude: 'Let me gulp that red
stuff ...that red stuff there'. Jacob saw his opportunity; a glint came
into his eye and he demanded the birthright in exchange. A rotten
thing to do. But Esau wasn't bothered: 'What profit will this birthright
bring to me?' Thus Esau despised the covenant promises of God and
opted rather for a plate of porridge! For this he is held up in Hebrews
as profane: a godless and bitter man (Hebrews 12.16). Seems daft, but
this is the mark of the man of the world because in the end all material

things are only a plate of porridge (remember Bunyan's man with the muck-rake!) Worldliness springs from an attitude to God and to material things: 'Give me pleasure now, I'm not going to wait for pie in the sky'.

But this incident is preceded by the judgement of God on the twins before their birth. God stated that there would be a division between them (23). Difficulties arise from the interpretation Paul gives to this. Quoting Malachi he wrote: '…before they were born, neither having done good or evil, God said; 'Jacob have I loved and Esau have I hated" (Romans 9.11). Now the first thing to realise is that the real mystery is why Jacob was loved and not why Esau was hated. All men are sinners and deserve the hatred of a holy God, yet God extends mercy. This is the basic mystery. Some attempt to explain the choice of Jacob by God by arguing that this was based on the attitude He knew the boys would take towards Him later in life. Yet Paul seems to exclude this by stating in Romans 9.11 that the purposes of God by election stand, and this has nothing to do with works or, presumably, attitude. Nevertheless, no matter how we see this paradox, and whether or not we attempt to resolve it, Scripture is absolutely clear that we must accept and teach that the eternal destiny of a man will be based on his own response to the offer of salvation in Christ. 'He that believes not is condemned ….because he has not believed' (John 3.18) and 'if any man hear My words and believe not, I judge him not, …the word I have spoken shall judge him in the last day (John 12.48).

A masterpiece of storytelling follows (chapter 27). Isaac was neurotic and for about forty years he thought he was dying and he makes frequent mention of his end! So he prepares to give his blessing, and despite his knowledge of God's selection, he says he will give his special blessing to Esau, his favourite son. He wants a nice setting and so he sends Esau out hunting. Rebecca overhears and immediately alerts Jacob, her favourite son, and schemes with him how to steal the blessing.

This family had been divided by this kind of favouritism, but now it is split irrevocably: the father selecting Esau for special treatment and the mother helping Jacob in his deceit. Because of it, Esau becomes murderous in his heart and Jacob has to flee, never to see his parents again.

Isaac makes a pathetic figure sitting and waiting for Esau to bring him a plate of venison. He is half blind and he doesn't notice when he is given kid. (Is this the origin of the phrase 'to kid someone'?) He is surprised that the chase has been so quick but Jacob tells him (20) that God had helped him! The old man is puzzled by the voice but he is reassured by the feel and the smell, which are those of Esau. He turns to the meal and gorges on the kid meat. Let us learn that our senses can deceive us and let us bring our natural desires for meat (or for a bit of flesh!) under control and not let them rule us. We can call on the help of the Holy Spirit in such situations, so never let us plead: '...but I'm only human'.

Stuffed with kid's meat, Isaac blesses Jacob, thinking it is Esau. And what a blessing - all about power and material success (28,29). No mention of God, no reference to His promises, or to the covenant. An old man, near to death, at the door of eternity, and yet he is occupied with food and material things.

Esau of course was furious when he returned from having caught his deer. 'I have been Jacob-ed (supplanted) he cries: Have you not reserved a blessing, even one blessing for me my father?' (36). And what a blessing he receives: 'Your dwelling will be away from the earth's richness ...you will live by the sword ...you will serve your brother' (39,40). Esau might well have been better without such a blessing!

What a contrast these blessings of Isaac make with the final writings of other saints. And what a contrast Isaac himself makes with the old saint who, in 1538, prayed:

'God be in my head, and in my understanding... God be at my end, and at my departing'.

11

THE HOUSE OF GOD

Jacob at Bethel
Genesis 28 NIV

Jacob has had to leave home and he spends his first night away in the open plain, with a stone as a pillow. He has a vivid dream and when he awakens, he says: 'Surely the Lord is in this place and I was not aware of it. This is none other than the house of God, this is the gate of heaven'. And he called the place Bethel, the house of God (16,17,19).

In the beginning of this chapter evidence of division multiply within the family of Isaac. The family is dysfunctional, torn apart by favouritism and destroyed by cheating and deceit. Jacob had deceived his father and for the second time he had tricked his brother (chapters 25 and 27). He was warned by his mother that Esau intended to kill him and she advised him to go away to his Uncle Laban 'for a few days', until Esau's anger would subside. Rebecca would then send for him and he could return. Deception however has become such a way of life within this family that Rebecca doesn't even come clean with her husband, but she makes up a story about how she is disgusted with the local girls and what a disaster it would be if Jacob married one of them. He must seek a wife elsewhere.

So Isaac sends Jacob away but before he goes he blesses him. Perhaps the one bright part in this whole sorry incident is that Isaac seems to acknowledge his mistake in having wanted to give the blessing to Esau. Isaac now warns Jacob to choose a wife with care because the promises of God are to be worked out through him. He therefore gives this son 'the blessing of Abraham' (4) and sends him away. This blessing is far more full that the one he had given earlier, but it still makes no mention of the covenant, nor of the blessings to the nations which will come through their descendants.

Despite the 'few days' separation of which Rebecca had spoken, Jacob never saw his parents again. Esau, on the other hand, hears about the repeated blessing given to Jacob and perhaps in order to pay back his father, he goes out and deliberately marries a local girl (8). There are clear lessons for us in all of this - lessons about openness and integrity, and lessons about 'togetherness' with our partner in handling our children.

Picture the situation: Jacob, only a lad, leaving home in disgrace and in fear, having to find his way to relatives he had never met. He travels until nightfall, and then he beds down on the open ground with a stone as a pillow. And in a dream he sees a ladder reaching from earth to heaven, with angels going up and down. And in his dream Jacob is blessed, the Lord using some of the terms that Isaac had used, but adding to these, and adding, most significantly, that in his seed (? singular) all the families of the earth would be blessed (14). Was there a special significance in the use by God in this blessing of the word: 'families'? Jacob had just wrecked his own family, but One would come who would unite families eternally. God then assures Jacob that He will be with him and will not leave him, adding significantly: '...until I have dealt with you! (15).

In response to the communication from God, Jacob built an altar, and prayed. But what a prayer! God had promised blessings, and a safe return to his homeland, yet in response Jacob offered God a bargain: 'If You will be with me, if You give me bread, if, if, if ...then I will give you a tenth' (20-22). Some Christians seem to do much the same today, viewing their tithe at a fair return. Many men of the world also do much the same: I've lived a good life, I've never cheated or hurt anyone ...God will have to be fair to me in the next life! Twenty years later, Jacob prayed a very different prayer 'I am not worthy of the least of all the mercies and the truth which You have shown to Your servant...' (32.10).

But what did it all mean, the ladder and the angels ascending and descending? Throughout Scripture angels are presented as the executors of God's purposes, that is, they are engaged in the government of God. Can we take it that God was appealing to Jacob to bring his life under His government and become involved in His purposes? The response of Jacob would seem to indicate this.

Upon wakening Jacob was overcome with awe at the thought of God having been active right beside him and his response was to recognise 'the house of God' and 'the gate of heaven'. Both these phrases imply government. The household of a man (or of God) is those persons who acknowledge the authority of that man, and for whom he is responsible. Furthermore, the gate of an ancient city was where the government, the administration and the business of the city took place (hence Lot had sat in the gate of Sodom 19.1).

God seems to have been inviting Jacob to repent, to seek forgiveness, to sort himself out, and work out the will of God in his life. In fact, it took him twenty years and more to reach that point, and during the intervening years there was further deception and dishonesty. He could have learnt these lessons at home, but like most of us, he learnt the hard way, through making mistakes and enduring hardships. God had to take him the hard way, but he did sort himself out and in his dying blessing he acknowledged that God had been his Shepherd 'all his life long' and had redeemed him from all evil (48.15).

In all this, Jacob was like Peter. The Lord had tried to teach Peter over supper, but Peter was too full of himself even to listen to the Lord. And so, the Lord had had to lead Peter into temptation in the house of the High Priest, and there, as he had warmed himself at a fire, Peter had learnt the limits of his own resources. But the Lord had delivered him from the evil in that situation - He prayed for Peter, and his faith did not fail (Luke 22.32).

12

BIGAMY AND WORSE

Jacob's wives and mistresses
Genesis 29 NIV

*Jacob travels on to Harran, where Abraham had settled for a while
(11.31). And in Laban, his uncle, he met his match! Like most of us,
Jacob had to learn the hard way. God would have us learn from His
word, but we are hard and most us only learn in the rough school
of experience. Jacob had turned away from God at Bethel, and he
went on to be taught a lesson in cheating by Laban. In the end, after
twenty years of increasing bitterness and distrust, God had to say to
him: 'Get out, come back to Bethel (House of God) and meet with Me
there'. And even on the way back to Bethel, there was more duplicity.
Yet through it all, despite all the evil in his life, Jacob showed that he
acknowledged God as Sovereign, and that he valued God's promises and
His covenant. But it took twenty long years for him to sort things out.*

In Harran, Jacob arrives at a well and meets some shepherdesses,
including Rachael, Laban's daughter. He must have seemed quite a
dashing young man to them as he removed the heavy stone cover and
drew water for their flocks (10). No trace of the selfish cheat he had
been and would soon become again. Laban received him into his home
with Eastern courtesy, and after a month's probation, Laban agreed to
employ him. They agreed that Jacob would serve seven years for one of
Laban's daughters - a strange contract because normally a dowry was
given with a bride. But Laban would out-do Jacob not only in this, but

also in substituting Leah, his other daughter, for Rachael. To this day, this event is commemorated in Jewish weddings, and when the bride arrives at the synagogue the groom goes to the entrance, lifts the veil of the bride and inspects her before they proceed with the marriage!

The haste of Jacob in all of this is notable. After having known Rachael for only a month, he binds himself to virtual slavery for seven years for her (14,18). No getting to know the girl first, and no prayer for guidance. In fact, although we are not told the will of God in the whole matter, there are hints in the behaviour of the two sisters that Leah was the more godly, and it was she who bore Judah, the ancestor of Jesus. Nor is it indicated how the girls felt about the wheeling and dealing that went on for them, though later they did indicate their disgust by complaining that their father had sold them (31.14,15).

The defence Laban gave for his deception in substituting Leah in the marriage ceremony is memorable: 'It is not done for the younger to precede the older' (26). A major lesson for Jacob! This was precisely what he himself had done in stealing his father's blessing from his older brother. God is Sovereign and He can use the most unlikely methods. He can even use a rogue like Laban to teach a lesson to His servant!

Jacob is so blinded by love that he serves another seven years and wins the hand of Rachael. But what an unhappy home results. Two wives are certainly not to be recommended... let alone two mistresses! The jealousy of the two girls, and Rachael in particular, leads to a discarding of moral standards. One of them even barters a few vegetables for Jacob's attention at night (30.15,16) and in their competition to have children the girls persuade Jacob to sleep with their maids. Scripture is purely factual on all of this. All this is recorded, and though no comment is made, it is all utterly against God's commands for marriage - total commitment to one partner within a 'covenant of companionship' (Genesis 2.24 and see Malachi 2.14) NIV.

Perhaps one of the most moving parts of all this story, and a part from which we can all learn, is the naming of Leah's children. There was no companionship in Jacob's marriage, and Leah craved just that. He had sex with her, but there was no communion, and not even communication. Hence the distress she showed after each birth (29.31-35). After the first: 'Now my husband will love me'. After the second: 'Because the Lord knew that I was hated, He has given me this son'. And then: 'Now, this time, will my husband be joined to me'. And then, after bearing her fourth son, Judah, Leah finds her consolation in God: 'Now I will praise the Lord'.

Malachi uses the lovely term for marriage: 'a covenant of companionship' (2.14). The basic element in companionship is communication. Remember how God had made Abraham His friend by telling him about His intentions (Genesis 18.17-19) NIV, and how Jesus later declared that the disciples were His friends: '...because I have told you all things' (John 15.15) NIV. Let us resolve to make our partners our very best friends by communicating with them - and above all, by sharing the things of Christ with each other!

13

TWO CHEATS COMPETE

Jacob and Laban
Genesis 30, 31 NIV

Jacob's domestic situation continues to deteriorate. So he plots with his wives and they slip away secretly, taking their flocks, and the children. Laban pursues them and he rebukes Jacob. But Laban's main concern seems to be that his idols have gone missing!

It is little wonder that the sons of Jacob turned out to be as they did. They saw little integrity in their father, and little respect by him for their mother(s). There is no evidence that Jacob gave them instruction in the things of God, or told them much about His promises and His covenant. Later they showed little care for their father, and they lied to cover up their disposal of Joseph. Scripture warns that the sins of the father are visited on their children. We reap what we sow in our children's minds and hearts.

The situation at work also deteriorated for Jacob. He had worked for Laban for fourteen years and had nothing to show for it, other than many mouths to feed! Laban has shrewdly retained all the capital (the flocks) and so Jacob is totally dependent upon him. Jacob begins to feel the futility of life as a slave of Laban and so he says that he wants to leave and return to his home together with his family. In flowery, but totally insincere language (27-) Laban asks him to stay because '...the Lord has blessed me for your sake'. They agree however that Jacob will continue to work with Laban's flocks, but he will take for himself all the speckled animals. By selective breeding Jacob ensures that most of the animals born thereafter are speckled, and so he increased his own wealth greatly at the expense of Laban.

It then became obvious to Jacob that Laban's attitude had changed (31.2). The selfishness and dishonesty were sickening both men. And so God intervened and called Jacob: 'Get out. Enough of all the lying and cheating, come back to Bethel, where you made a vow to Me' (13). Jacob had forgotten that vow, or rather the bargain he had made, but God in grace respects even the most miserable response made to Him. God is patient. Having '...led him into temptation', He was now going to '...deliver him from evil'. Twenty years had been wasted, and yet not totally wasted because Jacob was at last learning what man is, and he would soon learn Who God is. It has been said: if a man is to learn who God is, let him go to Bethel and meet God; if a man is to learn what man is, let him go to Harran and meet Laban!

Aware of the growing hostility of Laban, Jacob called his wives to a secret meeting in the fields (31.4). He complains to them about the treatment he has received - choosing to ignore his own duplicity (4-12) and he claims that God had revealed to him the method of selective breeding by which he had enriched himself (10-13). Rachael and Leah join in his complains about Laban, saying that he had sold them in marriage (to Jacob of course) and they had received nothing. They wait until Laban is occupied elsewhere and they slip away, taking with them all that was theirs - and a bit more (19). What a way for Jacob to leave what had been his home for twenty years, and what a way to take away a man's daughters.

Laban pursued them. He is highly indignant and says that he could have taken revenge on Jacob, but God had warned him not to (26-29). He then accuses Jacob of theft – his household gods had gone missing. What follows is pure farce! Laban searches the tents and fails to find the wretched idols. Jacob then turns on him and blows his top. And all the time, Rachael had been sitting upon the stupid idols! She had excused herself from rising for her father because, she told him: 'I'm having a period'!

Tension rises between the men as Jacob makes one accusation after another. In the end it is Laban rather than Jacob who introduces some grace into the situation. He asks Jacob to make a covenant with him, and in somewhat exaggerated terms they call the place Mizpah: The Lord watch between thee and me while we are apart' (31.49). Perhaps however this incident is most memorable because of the way that Jacob - at long last - calls upon God: the God of Abraham and 'the Fear of my father Isaac'. We have already commented on this name for God and the way that it shows the attitude of reverence for God that Jacob had seen in his father.

A remarkable phrase occurs later: 'God has not beheld iniquity in Jacob' (Numbers 23.21). God is realistic and the phrase is not: There is no iniquity in Jacob. However God is merciful and Jacob later sought, and obtained mercy. His sin is covered, and God sees no iniquity. This is the only basis for peace for any man with God.

14

AN ENCOUNTER
WITH GOD

Jacob at Penuel
Genesis 32 NIV

Jacob had wrecked his family by deception and dishonesty. He had had to flee from home and he landed up with his uncle, Laban, and his two daughters. His lying and cheating had wrecked that home too, and again he had fled, taking Leah, Rachael and their eleven children with him. Laban pursued him and an ugly situation could have developed. Laban however had cooled it and the two had parted friends. But as Laban's men disappeared over the horizon Jacob turned to face another much more dangerous enemy.

Jacob was on his way back to Bethel. It had been at Bethel, on his first night away from home, that he had had a vision of God in a dream. God had invited him to come under his government and make Him Lord of his life. Jacob had been filled with awe by the vision, he had recognised that God had been speaking to him. But Jacob had wanted no interference, so he had erected a stone, called it 'the house of God' and, leaving it and God behind, he had gone on to his uncle in Harran. Twenty years later, God now spoke to him again: 'Come back to Bethel ...where you made a vow' (31.13).

Jacob however knew a basic principle of reconciliation which was taught later by Jesus (Matthew 5.23-25) - before seeking reconciliation with

God, be first reconciled with your brother. The sincerity of a man who comes to God will be shown by the attitude he shows to his fellow men, and one who sincerely wants to get right with God will first try to put things right with his brother. So, Jacob made a long detour to the south, where Esau lived.

As he approached the territory of Esau Jacob sent messengers ahead. These returned with alarm: 'Esau is on his way with 400 armed men' (6). Jacob is terrified and typically, he resorts to scheming. He divides his family into two parts, sends the parties in opposite directions, hoping that if Esau gets one group, the other will escape.

Then he prays. And his prayer shows that he has come a long way since his first prayer, twenty years earlier (28.20-22). No offer of a bargain now to God. No offer of a tenth if God would protect, feed and clothe him. The fear of death straightens out a man's thinking, and not only was Jacob afraid, but he had run out of scheming. He was at the end of his own resources. His prayer is quite remarkable: 'I am not worthy of the least of Your mercies, and of all the truth You have shown to Your servant'. The mention of truth by this arch deceiver and cheat speaks volumes! He certainly has learnt a lot! So he casts himself on the mercy of God, he pleads for deliverance and he humbly reminds God of the promises He had made in the vision of twenty years previously.

But his scheming is not yet finished. He takes some of his goats, puts a drover in charge and sent them to meet Esau. As soon as they had gone, he took some ewes and dispatched them, then some camels etc., instructing each drover to say: 'A present to my Lord Esau from your servant Jacob'. His hope was that on receipt of present after present, Esau's anger would dissipate. But something more than this was happening. Years before Jacob had cheated Esau out of the blessing of their father. Now Jacob was returning more, probably much more than what would have constituted that blessing!

And Jacob was left alone (24). A significant phrase, because it is only when a man is alone and has exhausted all his own resources that God will truly meet with him. And yet, despite all his preparations a Man slipped through his defences and confronted him. They wrestled all night (24) and as morning broke the Man dislocated Jacob's hip (25). Jacob clung to the Stranger and evidently recognising something of the nature of this Man, he asked for a blessing. The Man asked him his name. Undoubtedly Jacob will have hung his head in shame at the question. Years before he had been asked his name by his father and he had denied that he was Jacob so that he could steal a blessing that was not his by right. Now he confesses: 'I am Jacob' (the supplanter). 'From now on', replied the Stranger, 'you will be called Israel, because you have striven with God' (28). When a man truly has an encounter with God he will cling to what he knows of God and will crave a blessing.

Jacob then asks the Stranger His name, but his request is refused (29). To a Hebrew, a name did not just mean the word by which they were called. Rather it summarised something of the character or the history of a person, or some outstanding characteristic or event. Was Christ, the Stranger who had wrestled with him, telling Jacob: 'You will only get to know Me now if you walk with Me, if you work out My Lordship day by day, situation by situation'. At the end of His life, Jesus said to his Father: 'I have declared Your name to My disciples' (John 17.6). That is, it had taken Jesus years of companionship before He could say that the disciples knew His name. So with us. We are given the opportunity to learn His name - His character, His nature - as we work out His Lordship in our lives, day by day, situation by situation.

As Jacob left the scene of the wrestling, he called it Penuel, because he said: 'I have seen God face to face' (30). He was a broken man, limping on a dislocated hip. What a state in which to meet the brother he had wronged! And yet he had never been stronger or more able to meet a situation, however threatening. He had had an encounter with God. He had been reconciled to God. He had been blessed by God and renamed by Him: 'One who strives with God, and with men' (28). Not that he was changed in that instant, rather Christ was saying: 'I give you a name to live up to: walk with Me and together we will gradually and painfully cleanse away the Jacob, and form something of the character of Christ in you'.

15

THE COST OF COMPROMISE

The massacre at Schechem
Genesis 33,34,35 NIV

*Jacob had been reconciled to God. At Penuel he had come to the
end of his resources and he had prayed for mercy. In a mysterious
encounter he had met with God - probably a Christophany, or pre-
incarnate appearance of Christ. He had confessed that he was Jacob,
the deceiver, and had been renamed Israel, one who strives with God.
He left Penuel and resumed his journey towards Esau, the brother
he had wronged. He was limping on a dislocated hip, but in truth
he had never been stronger. He had been blessed and renamed, and
he was now dependent upon God rather than his own craftiness.*

Jacob seems to have joined up with his family again and together they
journey towards Esau and his private army. The meeting between the
twins is dramatic! Esau ran to meet Jacob, embraced him and they
wept together. Jacob introduced his family and Esau asked about the
droves of cattle and sheep which had met him (33.8). Jacob explained
that they were a present. Esau then presses Jacob to come and stay with
him. The schemer emerges yet again in Jacob. He doesn't fully trust
Esau, yet he hasn't the courage to decline the invitation. So he makes
an excuse, telling Esau that they will all follow behind slowly '...until I
come to my lord Esau' (33.13). But as soon as Esau disappears, Jacob
immediately turns and goes the other way!

Jacob resumes his journey north towards Bethel. God had called him to return there '...where you made a vow' (31.13). Jacob was now retracing the steps Abraham had taken more than a hundred years before. Abraham had entered the land of promise at this same point, Shechem (12.7 and 33.18). But the difference was that Jacob settled in Shechem - short of Bethel, to which God had called him. He bought land there, spread his tent and settled down. And that compromise brought disaster. He was later to say that the conduct of his sons had 'made him to stink among the inhabitants of Shechem (34.30).

Alas, so many men go part way, and compromise their call from God. Only another twenty miles or so and he would have met with God at Bethel. In the same way, many men fail to respond fully to the call of God. They compromise, gradually their vision fades and they loose out - both in this life, and eternally! Amazingly, something like this seems to have worried Paul - of all people - and he writes a passage of exceptionally strong encouragement to the Corinthian church, ending with the fear that in the end he himself might be 'a castaway' (1 Corinthians 9. 24-27) NIV.

But what was wrong in settling in Shechem? It was a centre of trade, and jobs had to be found for the boys. Nothing wrong in trading cattle with the locals. So he built cattle sheds (33.17), bought some land (19) and settled in. Clearly he planned on staying, for the plot of land he bought was no back-yard. Later he gave it to Joseph, Joseph was buried there, and much later One who was much more famous that either Jacob or Joseph sat on the edge of a well there and talked to a Samaritan woman (John 4) NIV.

But the delay at Shechem led to rape, treachery and a massacre. Dinah, one of Jacob's daughters got friendly with some of the local women. One of the local princes fancied her and raped her. Jacob was evidently horrified but he said nothing about it. When his sons, Dina's brothers heard about it, they were furious. First, they made friendly overtures to the man who had offended, and to his father, even suggesting that they might intermarry with the locals 'and become one people with you' (34.16). Despite this, they plotted a terrible revenge, and three days later two of them, Simeon and Levi, led a massacre, taking as plunder everything in their houses.

Jacob was appalled, saying that his sons had made him to 'stink' among the inhabitants of the land. He never forgot the event, and on his deathbed, as part of his blessing(!) of his son, he said: Simeon and Levi and brethren: instruments of cruelty are in their habitations. O my soul, come not thou into their secret: unto their assembly, mine honour, be not thou united: for in their anger they slew a man, an in their selfwill they digged down a wall. Cursed be their anger, for it was fierce; and their wrath, for it was cruel: I will divide them in Jacob and scatter them in Israel'. (49.6,7) NIV.

The bottom line of the story however would seem to be that there is no limit to the degradation of a family in which there is no regular moral instruction and teaching in the things of God. What a contrast between Jacob in this, and Abraham who had been commended by God, because '...he will direct his children to keep the way of the Lord, by doing what is right and just' (18.19).

16

A HOME FOR GOD

Jacob returns to Bethel.
Genesis 35 NIV

Certain places come to have a special meaning for people. Bethel clearly became a very special place for Jacob. Gilgal became special for Joshua, Hebron for Caleb. It can be so for anyone - visiting the place of one's childhood can be an emotional experience for an exile, returning to a church where one had experienced something of God can be a most wholesome experience, married couples can find restoration in a return to the place of their honeymoon... and so on. And yet, while places and other things can be of symbolic value, they must not be allowed to obscure the real thing.

Bethel stood for everything that mattered to Jacob. God had first communicated to him there and for the rest of his life Bethel had acted like a magnet. Despite his imbalances and weaknesses Jacob had a love for God and a desire to get to know him. Sadly, his thirst for God was buried beneath layers of selfish desires. Yet the remembrance of God at Bethel drew him and he never forgot the vow he had made there as a young man (28.20-22). Twenty-five wasted years had passed and they had ended in disaster, with immorality, deceit, and, on the part of his sons, violence and murder. He had had success in every material way, he is wealthy and powerful, but his movements are watched with suspicion by surrounding hostile tribes.

And so Jacob obeys the call of God to come to Bethel (35.1). But he knew that things within his household were in no state for a meeting with God. And so he urged that they clean up ….and put away the strange gods that are among you. The wretched idols that Rachael had stolen from Laban were evidently still with them – surely a symptom of the state of the family. So they gave the idols to Jacob 'and Jacob hid them 'under the oak that was by Shechem' (35.4). Yet another act of compromise by Jacob. He hid the wretched things. Why didn't he destroy them? Did he have some lingering ideas that they might be useful, that there was some merit or some power in them, that God just might fail him and he might need them? He hid them and he noted the place.

Later, Moses showed us a much more appropriate way to deal with an idol or any other thing that would come between us and a full commitment to God, (see Exodus 32.20). The people had persuaded Aaron to make them a god, and out of their gold earrings he had made a golden calf. When Moses discovered this he ground the wretched gold calf to powder and strawed it upon the water (Exodus 32.20) so that it could never be reconstituted. And so the hymn writer wrote: '...*the dearest idol I have known, whate'er that idol be, help me to tear it from it's throne and worship only Thee.*

And so, following a further call from God, Jacob comes to Bethel, the House of God. No house or building of course. Just a place of memories and symbolism. But there Jacob brought himself under the government of God and was accepted into the household of God. He appears to have spent the rest of his life going round in a circle from Bethel to Haran, to Padan-aram, to Penuel, to Shechem and then back to Bethel. Yet it was not a circle, rather, it was a spiral. He had met with God at Penuel, he had cast himself on the mercy of God and he now came into a personal relationship with God. The spiral brought him ever closed to God, under his government.

50

And so, bethel became a special place for Jacob, and yet, places and things can become a distraction, or a substitute for the real thing. The nation of Israel later associated Bethel with mysticism and it seems to have degenerated into a place of idolatry. This led Amos to warn Israel: 'Seek not Bethel, nor enter into Gilgal, and pass not to Beersheba... for Bethel shall surely come to nought'. Rather, as Amos urges: 'Seek me and you shall live' (Amos 5.4,5).

17

JOSEPH'S UNHAPPY HOME

A social worker's nightmare!
Genesis 37 NIV

*And so Jacob settled down in Bethel with his family. Sadly, Jacob
had not learned much from either the good things or the bad
things in his own parents. On the one hand he went on to wreck
his family by showing favouritism to one son, and on the other
hand, he seems to have taught his sons little about God. The home
was torn apart by jealousies and by deception. In fact, the way
things in that home developed it was more than a case for referral
to a social worker - the police should have been called in!*

The trouble started with Joseph. He was a good lad, brighter and more
able than his brothers. That can be a difficult situation for a parent to
handle, but Jacob inflamed the situation greatly by showing Joseph
special favours. Joseph didn't help himself much either. He was a tell-
tale and he reported his brother's misdeed to their father. Then there
was the wretched coat. Apparently, such a coat would have been worn
by the leader of a tribe, so it was a provocative thing for Jacob to make
it and an ostentatious thing for Joseph to wear it, and Joseph seems to
strutted around in it, instead of hiding it away, or perhaps losing it!

No doubt all this was a consequence of the fact that Joseph, and his
younger brother Benjamin were the only sons of Rachael, Jacob's

favourite wife. The brothers had four mothers between them and - inevitably - there were endless jealous squabbles between them. Add to this the fact that Jacob seems to have given little teaching to his son's and practically no moral leadership. They grew up a violent and undisciplined lot. The committed murder and theft (34.25-30) and at least one of them was incestuous (38.15-18) NIV

And so Joseph, a man chosen by God for great things, grew up isolated and lonely. His mother was dead and everything his father did made things worse. No wonder he became a dreamer! Perhaps in his isolation he turned to fantasy ...one day, he'd show them! But No! All the indications are that Joseph had a keen interest in the things of God, and he seems to have questioned his father closely about the promises made by God to his ancestors. And in his dreaming, God spoke to him. His dreams are well known - the corn-sheaves of his brothers bowing down to him, followed by eleven stars, and then even the sun and the moon payid him obeisance! With an inexcusable lack of tact however: he told his brothers all about these dreams, and, surprise, surprise, they hated him all the more. Jacob rebuked the lad, though he took note of the dream (11).

God had great plans for Joseph. He was to be 'a saviour' of the world. But his home was so dreadful that he had to be taken away from it, both for his own protection and so that his character could develop and his knowledge of God grow. Furthermore, the arrogance and pride generated by his superior gifting and his father's favouritism, has to be purged away. Becoming a servant, fit for the Master's use would be a slow and painful process, but the phrase that occurs repeatedly as the story of Joseph unfolds is: 'And God was with him' – the phrase that Stephen highlighted later in his mention of Joseph in Acts 6.9 NIV.

And so, the brothers plot against Joseph and determine to kill him (37.19,20) NIV. Reuben, the oldest, makes a feeble plea for a compromise. Judah however asks what profit there is in killing the boy, and so they sell him to some long-distance lorry drivers. Then they kill a goat and stain the coat of Joseph with the blood and take it back to their father: 'Take it, and see if it is your son's robe', they coldly say (32). One's mind goes back to an earlier incident when Jacob himself had killed a goat in order to deceive his own father.

And so for the next twenty-five years the mills of God grind. God had to deal with the arrogance and ideas of self-importance of Joseph. He had to be brought low. God needed an administrator who would put the needs and interests of others before his own, and a man of absolute integrity.

And what about the brothers. For the next twenty-five years they had to live a lie, and their secret guilt must have destroyed relationships within their families. And in the end, they were found out! The story is well known, how once Joseph was assured that they had repented, he forgave the brothers. They then had to face their father and confess their deceit. Only then could attempts be made to start rebuilding relationships within the family.

But the family never really came together and Jacob stands in Scripture as perhaps the supreme example of a father who never assumed the role of head of his household. Unfaithful in marriage, he gave no moral or spiritual leadership to his family. One's mind goes back to a statement of Rabbi Jacobowitch when commenting on the stability of the Jewish nation: '...the Jews sanctify their homes as places where the Scriptures are central'.

And yet, Jacob had a thirst after God, and he came into a deep knowledge and relationship with God. But sadly this seems to have been at the end of his life, when all the vigour and energy of youth had been dissipated selfishly. Perhaps it is no accident that in Hebrews chapter11, which lists the great men of faith in the Old Testament, Jacob appears - but the incident which is referred to is right at the end of his life!

18

JOSEPH, A SLAVE IN POTIFER'S HOUSE

Potifer and his wife.
Genesis 39.10-23 NIV

In an interlude in the story of Joseph the writer introduces Potifer, a governor in Egypt, the Captain of the Guard. He had bought Joe as a slave, and he would be the instrument which God would use in preparing Joseph for His purposes. Potifer was clearly a kindly and honourable man, but his marriage had run out of steam, and he came home only for meals!

The main incident in this chapter is quite unremarkable. It can be seen any day on the television. The boss's wife sets out to seduce an attractive young man. She has been neglected by her husband. His career has taken him over and his marriage has come to mean little to him. Because of his neglect, marriage means little to her either. What makes the story different to a late-night movie and what gives it its supreme value for us, is that the woman does not succeed! The young man practices the presence of God and he has such a clear concept of right and wrong that nothing happens. Yet for all his integrity the young man is falsely accused and he ends up in prison. But even in prison, he practices the presence of God. The key phrase in this chapter, as in the whole of the life of Joseph is 'The Lord was with him', or, we might re-phrase it - Joseph was sensitive to the presence of the Lord with him at all times - and it showed in everything he did.

Why did Potiphar's wife become infatuated with Joseph? After all Joe was probably only one of many slaves in what was likely to have been a huge official residence, and she was the wife of a top civil servant. Perhaps the clue lies in the sentence: 'So Potiphar left everything in Joseph's charge and had no concern for anything other than the food he ate.'

Here is a man who took his wife for granted. His career was so absorbing and his work so interesting that he only came home for meals (39.6). Even when Joseph took over the running of the household and Potiphar had lots more free time, he spent it all outside the home. He made no attempt to put time or effort back into his marriage. He had every opportunity to rediscover the girl who had thrilled him once, and to gain a new understanding and a better rapport with her. There must have been many situations at work which would have benefited from a woman's knowledge and intuition. There must have been many things to do with the running of the household, and the bringing up of the children which Potiphar should have discussed with his wife. But no! No communication. No companionship. He only came home for meals!

No wonder the woman became infatuated with one of the slaves. She had become no more than the provider of food: she was no longer appreciated by her husband, she was neither valued nor fulfilled. Their marriage was bankrupt.

Do grasp the basic principle of marriage as ordained by God: companionship and communication! God gave marriage to man as a creation ordinance, and He gave it for man's highest good. One's partner is to have first place, after God, and commitment of each to the other is to be total. Sport, friends, work, and even children all too easily fill one's life at the expense of one's partner. The woman is especially vulnerable, and her life can so easily become drab and repetitive if her husband comes in only for his meals. This is particularly likely if the man is tired and uncommunicative when he does come home, and if he only wants to watch the wretched box, rather than tell her about his day (and what is even more important: ask her about her day!). No wonder depression is common amongst women, and no wonder some turn to drink and some to an illicit affair.

Scripture teaches that in the marriage partnership the man is the head. Whatever else headship means, it certainly means responsibility for the health of the marriage. To have no concern for anything at home other than food is no way to exercise headship, or preserve the health, the freshness, the joy, the satisfaction and the fulfilment of marriage. Companionship is the first and primary reason given in Scripture for marriage (Genesis 2.18-24). At the creation God stood as it were with His Hands on the shoulders of the first couple and blessed them, calling them 'help-meets', or companions for each other. No one who shrugs that hand off his marriage will be blessed by God.

Companionship is then stressed throughout the rest of the Bible. For example: Paul uses a most challenging phrase when he says 'Let the husband give unto the wife due benevolence, and likewise the wife unto the husband' (1 Corinthians 7.3). Bene-volente is simply Latin for 'well-wishing'. That is: the needs and the desires of one's partner should come first, and everything one does should be with the other partner in mind, and nothing that might be against hers, or his very best interests should be contemplated.

Potiphar's wife was lonely and neglected. Unvalued by her husband, she craved to be noticed, and to be wanted. So she turned to Joseph and, as one translation puts it: 'she eyed him (7). Unfaithfulness begins with the eye. We all know how the second look is often prompted by wrong thoughts, and how easily it can lead on to lustful looks. Jesus warned about the sin of looking lustfully at a woman (Matthew 5.27-29) and Peter warned about '...pleasure seekers with eyes full of adultery' (2 Peter 2.14) NIV.

Marriage is a creation ordinance and the rules apply to all couples, and not just to Christians. Like some men today, Potiphar's wife regarded her marriage to Pothiphar as a frustration, a bondage that could be broken out of with no great worry. She no doubt pleaded with Joseph ...my husband only comes home for meals ...it doesn't matter ...he won't care. But marriage is a sacred covenant before God, whether or not God is acknowledged in the ceremony. It is a creation ordinance, given by God at the creation of man. Joseph therefore did not argue '...but we dare not ...Potiphar might find out'. Rather he stated that what she was suggesting was a great wickedness, a sin against God' (9).

Sadly, even Christian marriages get into difficulties, and for some things start to go wrong because of exactly the same neglect that Potiphar showed to his wife. Peter used a beautiful phrase about Christian married couples: he wrote that they are 'heirs together of the grace of life' (1 Peter 3.7). Sadly, many couples fail to enter into this inheritance together, making it a practice to share the things of Christ with each other. Those who don't are losers - and their loss will be eternal!

19

JOSEPH IN PRISON

'…and the Lord was with him.'
Genesis 39, 40 NIV

It is a common mistake to expect that a good life will necessarily be rewarded in terms of peace and plenty. It often is, but the purposes of God in a man's life are often far more grand and more complex than anything we could ever imagine. When disaster strikes, and particularly if this is believed to be undeserved, we should ask "(Lord, what are you teaching me …what are you preparing me for?)' Sadly we usually react: 'Why me … what have I done to deserve this?' The way Joseph reacted to disaster - the second major undeserved tragedy in his life - is a lesson for us all.

Joseph was greatly wronged by a spiteful woman. He had been chief steward in the house of Potiphar, an Egyptian official. Potiphar's wife, neglected by her husband, had made eyes at Joseph (7). Joseph had maintained his integrity even though she had attempted to seduce him by force (11,12). The seductress then became a vengeful she-cat and denounced Joseph to Potiphar.

Potiphar seems to have had doubts about the reliability of his wife. The penalty for adultery was death, yet Joseph was only put in prison, and the king's prison at that. By far the most remarkable thing at this point of the story however is the silence of Joseph. Why did he not defend himself? He was no weed and yet he said nothing. Until this incident had occurred Potiphar had found Joseph to be totally reliable and surely he would have listened to Joseph. But no! Joseph made no attempt to defend himself, and as a consequence he suffered unjustly. To an extent he brought it on himself!

Why did Joseph remain silent? Clearly it was because he had a most exalted view of marriage. There was little left of Potiphar's marriage: Potiphar was a workaholic who only came home for meals (6). But the woman was still his wife and marriage is sacred. Joseph knew that had he spoken out, had he told Potiphar what his wife had really done, the marriage would have been destroyed. Was it out of respect for marriage as an ordinance of Almighty God, that Joseph held his peace and suffered in silence?

We can all learn from this. How quick we are to jump to our defence. Our concept of the truth drives us to plead to argue and perhaps even to fight for our version of what really happened! But how much more noticeable all this is when the truth is in our favour, and yet, most of us show a lot less concern about what really happened when we have been at fault ourselves. In other words, most of us are really concerned with number one rather than with the truth! But even when we have been in the right, we often fight for the truth with little or no concern for wider issues. Joseph could well have said: 'Blow her and everyone else - I demand justice, I will have my rights!' But he didn't. He thought first, and he realised that a marriage was at stake.

Let's learn from Joseph. It usually is right and proper for us to speak out, but there are occasions when there are bigger issues involved than simply our good name, or our own standing. In fact we have a far greater example than Joseph and in his first letter, Peter draws on this in his first letter. Jesus Christ suffered unjustly, He was unfairly condemned - and yet He remained silent. As the prophesy put it: He was oppressed and He was afflicted, yet He opened not His mouth (Isaiah: 53.6). And Peter points out: 'He left us an example' (1. Peter 2.21-25). Just think of it: where would we be if Jesus had argued the truth and had spoken up for His rights as an innocent victim of undeserved hatred? There was an infinitely greater issue at stake than His standing before the Jews or the Romans, and so He kept silent.

But the example of Jesus is of immense importance to us because Peter, in drawing on his example, gives the final conclusion on the whole matter of unjust and unmerited suffering. Again, holding up Christ as our example, Peter says: "…He committed Himself to Him Who judges righteously' (1 Peter 2.23). For the Christian, there is another world in which right will triumph and justice will be done. There is a God of Truth. Nothing is hidden from Him, and He will recompense those who have suffered without cause. He is The God of Recompenses. Just as punishment for sin is a constant theme throughout the Bible, so recompense is also a repeated theme, and words for recompense are used over fifty times.

Say to those who are of a fearful heart: "Be strong, fear not! Behold your God will come with vengeance and with recompense. He will come and save you.' (Isaiah 35.4) 'Vengeance is Mine, and recompense …for the Lord will vindicate His people and have compassion on His servants' (Deuteronomy 32 35,36) NIV.

The other thing about suffering is that God always has a purpose. We will seldom be able to discern this because His purposes are complex. But He is not a capricious God: everything has a cause and an effect, and He is ultimately sovereign of both. In the case of Joseph we know how it all turned out. He was vindicated: he became ruler of Egypt, second only to Pharaoh, and he became the saviour of the nation. Yet to see only this is to miss the point: it was not simply that the undeserved sufferings of Joseph were recompensed later, the even more important point is that God was in those situations with Joseph, fitting him for his role in God's own purposes. Psalm 105.17,18 is probably making this very point when it says that in the sufferings of Joseph 'he was laid in iron', which we might paraphrase: he became a man of steel. God was preparing Joseph for the enormous task of ruling a major nation during a time of famine and profound social upheaval. In the task of building up colossal stores of food, and later in co-ordinating a massive famine relief scheme, Joseph would need an iron will, and an inflexible integrity. He learnt these, and more, in the prison.

But first, Joseph had to be sorted out. God had to deal with two particular imbalances in the character of Joseph: self-importance and self-pity. The first was an obvious consequence of the favouritism and spoiling by his father. And because of it Joseph had to be brought low and he became a slave. Society teaches men to stand up for their rights, and one who accepts a lowly position, or an injustice without complaint is dismissed as a mere wimp. Had Joseph retained a 'spoilt boy' attitude slavery would have crushed him. But God was training an administrator and leader who would put the needs of others before his own. One who is concerned with his own 'rights' is of no use to God, and, after all, we have the supreme example of Christ Himself (Philippians 2).

The other possible outcome of Joseph's situation could have been self-pity. Life hadn't been fair. He hadn't done anything to deserve all this. And so he could have become bitter and resentful, sullen and hostile. Had he done so, again slavery would have crushed him. But God needed a servant who was in full control of his senses and his emotions, and one who would serve the Lord Christ and work honourably in front of his master, and behind his back.

20

THE STEPS TO THE THRONE

The sons of Joseph: 'Forgetting' and 'Fruitful'
Genesis 41 NIV

Joseph had two children. The first he called Manasseh, 'because God has made me forget all my toil and all my father's house' (41.51). And he called his second son Ephraim, because, 'God has caused me to be fruitful in the land of my affliction' (41.52). A whole life summarised in the names of two lads!

Joseph had two companions in prison. Each of them had a dream and under the guidance of God Joseph had given each an interpretation. One interpretation had been good, and after he had given this, Joseph had added a plea for himself: 'Make mention of me to Pharoah and bring me out of this place' (40.14).

Some commentators have reacted sharply to this request of Joseph saying that he should not have asked for such a favour. His trust should have been in God alone and having pleaded his case at the Throne of Grace he should have left it there with the One Who judges righteously. This is not for us to judge. Suffice it to say that it was a most human thing for him to do. Falsely accused and wrongfully imprisoned, who would not have sought justice by whatever means became available.

Whatever we feel about this, we can be absolutely certain that God was in control of the situation and in a most remarkable way He used the forgetfulness of the butler to achieve His own great purposes. This is a remarkable aspect of the Sovereignty of God: He uses the failings of men, and even their faults, to achieve His purposes. (See Acts 4.27,28 for the most remarkable example of this.)

The butler forgot his promise (40.23) and Joseph was left in prison for a further two years (41.1). But just consider what might have happened if Joseph's friend had managed to get him released. Joseph could well have been seriously indebted to the butler, and he could have been exploited by the butler for his own purposes. God had much greater things for Joseph: but they had to wait His timing, and God used even the forgetfulness of the butler to achieve His purposes.

Let none of this encourage us to regard any of our own promises lightly. Is there someone to whom we said we would write, or visit, or do some favour, and we forgot? It is never too late to redeem such promises, and perhaps we will find that in the carrying out of our word long afterwards there is added blessing. Jesus warned that if we don't, we will be judged in the end for even our 'idle' words (Matthew 12.36), that is, things we have said lightly with little real intent. What a shame if some of these light things were promises to others, promises made with no real intention of fulfilment. Be dependable, be men of your word. Jesus said: 'let your 'Yes' be Yes and your 'No' No'.

Then Pharaoh had a dream. The Egyptians were steeped in astrology and in the reading of omens of all kinds - not unlike some today! The dream worried Pharaoh (8) and so he called his magicians and told it to them. They had no explanation.

Then the chief butler remembered Joseph back in the prison cell (9). The concern of Pharaoh is shown in the statement that Joseph was brought 'hastily' (literally: brought running!). The calm of Joseph as he stands before Pharaoh is remarkable: 'It is not in me' he says, 'but God will give Pharaoh an answer of peace (16). In fact the interpretation he gives appears with hindsight to be somewhat obvious. Moreover he goes on to give Pharaoh advice which again with hindsight seems to be common sense. However, considering the stress Joseph must have been under, his shrewdness and balance is remarkable, and one is reminded of our Lord's promise in Matthew 10.18,19.

There were to be seven years of unusual plenty followed by seven years of severe famine. 'Levy a tax of one-fifth of all the crops during those years of plenty' advised Joseph. 'Store the excess in granaries throughout the land and release it during the years of famine. And' added Joseph 'put the administration of all this under a man who is wise and dependable.' Pharaoh saw in Joseph the man with the qualities required for the task and so, without any delay, he appointed him (39-45). In addition to immense material benefits Joseph was given an Egyptian name which has been variously translated as "Preserver of Life', or 'The one who furnishes the nourishment of life'.

There has been much criticism of Joseph for the capitalism' he introduced. The taxing of the people during the time of plenty (48,49) is seen as acceptable, and the selling of the grain once the famine commenced (56) is seen as reasonable. Later however, Joseph caused the people to surrender their land to Pharaoh, and the whole structure of Egyptian society was radically changed (47.13-26). This last, the critics say, was going too far and was nothing less than capitalist exploitation. It has however been pointed out that the whole agricultural system of Egypt up to this time was unorganised and highly unstable, and around this time a complete system of storage lakes and irrigation canals were dug. These, and the maintenance of the various waterways will have required vast sums of money, and this is exactly what the taxation system of Joseph would have provided.

It would be impossible to adequately portray the change in Joseph's fortunes. From being neglected and forgotten in prison, he found himself, within hours, ruler of the most wealthy country of his day.

He must have been exposed to numerous temptations. How easy it would have been for him to become materialistic and to lapse into paganism ...and there were some old scores to be settled!

But Joseph was still obedient to God and he still maintained his standards. God had been with Him during his slavery and while in prison (rather, as we repeatedly emphasise: Joseph was sensitive to God's Presence with him). His unquestioning obedience to God had kept him from sin, from disbelief and from despair while in the house of Potiphar and in prison. Now, his submission to God prevented him from becoming proud and arrogant. Rather, he set aside the memory of all he had suffered (hence 'Manasseh') and he rejoiced in the opportunities to serve and benefit others (hence 'Ephraim').

21

JOSEPH MEETS HIS BROTHERS AGAIN

He begins to challenge them.
Genesis 42 NIV

As the story of Joseph and his family develops, a number of issue basic to relationships are dealt with. Do you have difficulties understanding conscience, guilt, repentance, forgiveness, reconciliation and restoration? The story of Joseph in chapters 42-45 will help understand these, but the length of the narrative indicates how important and yet how difficult these issues are.

Over twenty years have passed since Joseph had been sold by his brothers to the slave dealers. Joseph will have been devastated by the heartlessness of his brothers, and he will have suffered mental torment at being torn from all he knew and thrown into slavery in a foreign city. Joseph however came to terms with his situation and we have seen how, despite further terrible injustices, he had avoided becoming bitter or resentful, and God had therefore been able to use him.

Many a life has been spoilt by a wrong suffered innocently. But the greatest harm can be done not by the wrong itself, but by the spirit of resentment which has been allowed to develop and which has been fostered, perhaps for the rest of life – like Burn's sulky sullen dame who sat 'nursing her wrath to keep it warm'! Like Joseph, the Christian has a way of dealing with the wrongs he has suffered innocently. He can take them, as a deliberate act of the mind and will, and commit them to the One Who judges righteously (1 Peter 2.23). It this is not done then past wrongs can fester and can cause terrible harm to the one who has been wronged, while doing nothing to the perpetrator of the wrong!

But the sufferings of Joseph are now over. He has been taken out of prison and exalted next to the throne. Because of the wisdom he had shown Pharaoh has proclaimed the supremacy of Joseph to all the people: "Can we find such a one, a man in whom the Spirit of God is? ... you shall be over my house ...according to your word shall all my people be ruled (41.38-40). And in due course, the brothers of Joseph fulfil his early dreams when the come and bow down to him!

The famine which Joseph had predicted from the dream of Pharaoh had begun, and after a few years it started to bite. This famine was unusual in that it affected many countries. Word spread however that there was a grain mountain in Egypt and all the earth came to Egypt to buy grain' (41.57).

When Jacob heard that there was grain in Egypt, he said to his sons ...go down and buy grain for us there, that we may live and not die' (42.1). The mention of Egypt had an immediate effect – the brothers froze! Jacob sensed their embarrassment: 'Why do you just look at one another? (42.1) he asked. Clearly, their consciences were at work.

Jacob evidently had some difficulty in persuading them to go to Egypt, but in the end ten hungry men went to Egypt in search of food. They came to the Governor of Egypt, not knowing that it was Joseph, and they bowed down to him. Joseph recognised them ...and he remembered his dreams of over twenty years before (6,9). He had had to wait a very long time, but God is faithful and what had been foretold in his boyhood dreams now came to pass.

Joseph knew his brothers immediately. What was he to do? What a chance to take his revenge! But no! He had committed the wrongs he had suffered to the one who judges righteously and there is never any trace of bitterness or anger in anything Joseph said or did.

He could have ignored them. After all, they had never wanted him. He owed them nothing and he was now happily settled in Egypt. Why bother? Give them food and let them go! But no! Love isn't like that. Relationships cannot be picked up and dropped lightly. They were his flesh and blood, and his heart went out to them. Furthermore, Joseph wanted to give the brothers, and the whole family, something to live for, not just something to live on.

He could forgive and forget. Why go over it all now. He had done well and he could afford to be big-hearted. Embrace each of them and let bygones be bygones. But No! There would always be that awful skeleton in the cupboard and it would haunt them until they faced it and dealt with it. And there was the whole network of lies and deception of their father and their wives back home. There could be no brushing what they had done under the carpet and pretending that it had never happened.

Or he could work towards reconciliation. If the family was ever to come together, if suspicions were to be ended, if relationships were to be healed, then the brothers would have to face themselves and their past. They would have to be reconciled with the brother they had wronged and with the father they had deceived. In no way could they atone for what they had done, but they could be forgiven. Genuine and secure relationships could be built up, but these would only be possible if there was forgiveness on the part of Joseph and his father, and for that to be real there had to be repentance and a change of heart on the part of the brothers.

So Joseph did not reveal who he was. To have done so would have achieved nothing at this stage. Rather, he treated his brothers severely, accusing them of being spies. Very early in the defence the brothers made to this charge it must have become obvious to Joseph that they were still intent on covering up the past. There was no hint of repentance in the way they spoke about their family. 'Your servants are twelve brothers, the sons of one man ... the youngest is with our father, and one is no more' (12). Just imagine - the brothers standing in front of Joseph telling him that he was no more! Joseph did learn however that his father was still alive - no doubt his heart missed another beat.

What a dramatic moment. Standing before the man who had complete power and authority over them, the one man who knew all about them, the one man who could help them, and who was intensely anxious to do them good - and they say "...he is not'. Another most bizzare statement the brothers made in their defence was 'Your servants are not spies ...we are honest men' (11). Honest men indeed - how ever did Joseph restrain himself and keep his cool?

It was therefore abundantly clear to Joseph that whatever regrets the brothers might have had about what they had done, they had not begun to repent. There was no change of heart. They would continue to repress the whole incident and would continue to live a lie for the rest of their lives. If Joseph was to achieve anything with them, if he was going to unite the family, he would have to bring them to repentance. And unless he could achieve this, there would be no point in revealing himself. There was no place for forgiving and forgetting', or just brushing the whole thing under the carpet. The family was torn apart by past evils and continuing lies and deception. It would have been so easy for Joseph just to give them corn and let them go. But this would only have given the family something to live on: Joseph knew that they desperately needed something to live for.

How like God Joseph is in all of this. God has complete power and authority, He knows everything about each one of us, He is the one who can, and intensely desires to help us, - and yet men say ...'He is not'. And those who do acknowledge His existence see only the severe side of His severe side of His dealings with us: '....if God is love why does He do this ...why does He permit this ...if there is a God at all why doesn't He stop that' and so on.

Yet God cannot brush things under the carpet any more than Joseph could. He must bring us to a change of heart if we are to be brought into a relationship with Himself. Hence we sometimes speak of the severe mercy of God. He is not willing that any should perish and so He works for our salvation and we all know how ease and comfort will never bring us to repentance. It is in times of difficulty that we are most aware of our need for God. So yet again, Joseph stands as God in this story, as the brothers stand before him without recognising who he is, and they see only his harshness and not his tears (24).

22

THEIR CONSCIENCES AWAKENED

'What is God doing to us?'
Genesis 42-43 NIV

In his 'severe mercy' Joseph gives the brothers a taste of their own medicine. Not in any sense to pay them back, but to remind them of how they had behaved, to stimulate their consciences and to challenge them to face what they had done.

Joseph had the brothers put in prison for three days (17) and then he challenged them to verify their story about a brother back home. 'If you are honest men, let one of your brothers stay here in prison, while the rest of you go and take grain back for your starving households. But you must bring your youngest brother to me, so that your words may be verified and that you may not die.' (42.19,20 NIV). In this way he re-enacted the events of twenty years earlier. Would the brothers desert Simeon, the one held in prison. Would they make up some cock and bull story for their father as an explanation of their return without him, or would their consciences be awakened, and would their behaviour be more honourable this time?

The answer came almost immediately. Their consciences began to trouble them. Despite over twenty years of cover-up that terrible deed was locked in their memories, and it now flashed before them in absolute clarity. They began to say to each other (in Hebrew, thinking that Joseph would not understand!) 'In truth we are guilty concerning our brother, in that we saw the distress of his soul, when he besought us and we would not listen; therefore is this distress come upon us' (21). And as often happens in such situations, one brother began to lament that the others had not listened to him, implying blame on the others. If only they had listened, then this reckoning for his blood would not have come upon us (22). Reuben was correct in what he said; he had urged the others not to harm Joseph (37.21.22), yet in the end Reuben had gone along with the others and he was therefore just as guilty as the others.

So nine brothers leave Egypt and start the journey back home. Their minds must have been in a turmoil. The simple visit to Egypt for corn had become complicated beyond anything they could ever have imagined, and how would they face their father without Simeon? With heavy hearts they travelled to the first stopping place on the road back home. And as one of them took some of the Egyptian corn from a sack to give to his animal he sees the money they had paid for it in the mouth of the sack. In alarm he calls the others: My money is returned, and their hearts missed a beat! But then they say a most significant thing to each other: 'What is this that God has done to us' (42.28 NIV).

The brothers return to Jacob and tell him all. Jacob laments that they had mentioned that they had another brother, and he refuses flatly to let Benjamin go with them. But when they had eaten the corn which they had brought out of Egypt Reuben offers, in a most noble speech, to go surety for Benjamin (43.8,9). Jacob relents and tells them to take the man a present – the best fruits in the land, a little balm, honey, spices, myrrh, nuts and almonds…. and take double money in your hand.

The last test Joseph devised revealed the deepest thoughts and intents of the brothers. He sent them on their way home, again laden with corn, but he told his servant to put his silver cup into the sack of Benjamin. The brothers set off, no doubt highly relieved that they were all together, unscathed. Before they had gone very far however, they were pursued by Joseph's steward. "Why have you taken my master's cup?" he asks. The brothers are aghast. What nonsense: why would any of us do such a thing. They let down their sacks and open them, beginning with that of the eldest. Imagine their horror when the cup is found in the sack of Benjamin, the youngest!

Now if the men had not changed, we can imagine their reaction: 'What: Benjamin! Father's pet! You're a right rotter! You can take all that's coming!' But no, the brothers are utterly changed. They all return together, and when they meet Joseph they confess that God has found them out and we are all now your slaves'. And then Judah, who had formerly been perhaps the most cruel and selfish of all the brothers, pleaded for Benjamin and offered himself as a substitute in one of the most noble speeches in the whole of Genesis (44.18-34).

So Joseph is assured of their repentance. The brothers don't just regret the past: they have turned completely from their former evil ways, and their loving treatment of Benjamin gives evidence of their change of heart. Joseph is so moved that he weeps, tells them who he is, and freely forgives them (45.1-15).

But the best part of the story is still to come. Forgiveness is not just a negative: putting away admitting and facing the wrongs of the past, there are positive effects of forgiveness. The relationship between Joseph and his brothers was restored, the family was united again, they had all something to live for again.

And so it is with man and God. Forgiveness is a free gift from God. We can do nothing to earn it and we certainly don't deserve it. It is offered as a free gift. But it cost God His Beloved Son and the cross stands for ever as the basis for our forgiveness. Two alternatives face each one of us. If we repent and seek forgiveness we will enjoy eternal life with God: if we reject or ignore God's free offer we will spend eternity shut out from God. There are only these two choices and these two destinies.

God so loved us that He sent His Only Son, so that whoever believes in Him will not perish but have everlasting life. John 3.16 NIV

23

RECONCILLIATION

Relationships restored.
Genesis 44,45

When Joseph saw that his brothers had changed and had truly repented, he was himself overcome with emotion. He wept, indeed he was overcome with weeping. He told his servants to leave them, and as soon as they are gone he tells them 'I am your brother Joseph - Come unto me'. Many years later, another said: 'Come unto me all you who are heavy laden, and you will find rest (Matthew 11.28) KJV.

The brothers were incredulous! Actually, they must have been terrified at first (3). The past had caught up with them. They will not have believed that their own brother was standing before them ...and would he accuse then or was he really offering forgiveness? Joseph didn't condemn them, but neither did he dismiss what they had done. Real forgiveness demands that the past is faced, and not lightly dismissed. 'You sold me', he said, but God was in it all, He was sending me to Egypt so that I would be able to save many lives (5).

Then when they were calm and reassured, he embraced each of them ...and they talked together (15). That must have been some conversation! From being fearful and apprehensive at first they will have become relaxed and their tongues will have been loosed as they realised how genuine Joseph's forgiveness was. They will have talked far into the night.

Restoring relationships after a wrong has been committed is not easy, and hence the long and difficult process Joseph had to go through before he could reveal himself to his brothers. In his teaching on relationships Jesus suggested a three-stage process in handling an offence and attempting to 'gain your brother' (Matthew 18.15-17 NIV).

Joseph had gained his brothers, but the best is yet to come. He said to his brothers: Go home, fetch Dad and your families, and then come, live with me and be near me' (10). In this, the hope of the Christian is beautifully illustrated. Before Jesus left this earth He said: I am going to prepare a place in heaven for you, and I will come again and take you to be with me for ever' (John 14.3).

Perhaps the most surprising statement in this part of the story is when Joseph tells his brothers to go home and collect their families, "...but don't bother about your own stuff: the best of the land here will be yours (20). Just think of it - all the possessions the brothers had collected, for some of which they had worked, but others for which they had lied and cheated, and for some they had even killed - they were to leave it all behind! What? All the things they had treasured and valued - it was all of no consequence in the end? So it will be for each of us one day. We will leave it all behind! No wonder Jesus warned us not to build up treasure on earth, but lay up for yourselves treasure in heaven.

In most disagreements or difference of any kind, it is usually necessary for both those involved to compromise if reconciliation is to be achieved. Both have to give a little so that they can meet in the middle. But the Bible makes it clear that reconciliation between man and God is utterly different to this. God cannot change. His standards of purity and holiness are absolute. If He compromised His standards then He would cease to be God. Hence the Bible urges: 'Be reconciled to God' (2 Corinthians 5.20 NIV). All the change has to be on the part of man. Yet man cannot lift himself up to God. Man's works cannot atone for sin, and nothing that we can do can wipe away one sin. God had to provide the means for man's reconciliation, and this He did in the death of His Son, Jesus Christ.

24

THE DEATH OF JACOB

He worshipped, leaning on his staff.
Genesis 48,49 KJV

The writer of the book of Hebrews wrote some brilliant thumb-nail'
biographies. One of his masterpieces is that of Jacob. In only a single
verse he managed to encapsulate a lifetime's experience of God: 'By
faith Jacob, when he was a-dying, blessed both the sons of Joseph, and
worshipped, leaning on the top of his staff.' (Hebrews 11.21 KJV)

Jacob knew that his end was near and as a final act he called his sons together and blessed them. Weak in body but strong in spirit and filled with confidence in the promises of God, the dying Patriarch witnessed to what he had learnt of the faithfulness of God. And it is in this that the value of these chapter lies. Most of us can identify with Jacob. He had been a man of tremendous potential and under God he could have achieved great things but sadly, in the end he achieved little. He did however get to know the mercy and the goodness of God in a unique way and he acknowledged this in his dying blessings of his sons. If only, during his most active days Jacob had been half the man he was on his death-bed, his story would have been very different! Let us learn - these things were written for our warning and our encouragement (1 Corinthians 10.11).

The old man is an exile in a strange country. He knows he is dying and he is apprehensive for his sons. In the past they had not shown themselves to be honourable in their dealings with others. Now they have settled in Egypt as shepherds, and as such they will be despised by the Egyptians. Furthermore, they are surrounded by an idolatrous, sun-worshipping race, an there is a strong likelihood that they will depart from the worship of God. Jacob's apprehension for them must have been heightened by the knowledge that he himself had done little to teach his family about God. So he calls them to his bedside to hear his dying warnings and encouragements.

The terms in which Jacob blesses each son are remarkable. Several of the blessings draw upon events in the past in which a son had shown some character trait, and Jacob predicts how that trait will develop and show later as a national characteristic. Some of the blessings are prophetic, and that given to Judah is especially memorable as it focussed upon the coming Messiah and several phrases Jacob used are repeated later with application to Christ.

The way this incident is described (from the last verse of chapter 47 to 48.21) it makes a most moving picture. The old man heaves himself up on his bed, calls for his staff and leans on it (47.31). He tells Joseph that he is going to bless his two grandsons. He begins to ramble ...as for me, when I came from Padan, Rachael died ... and typical of an old man he goes off on a long digression about Rachael, his beloved wife. Then he comes to, and with a start he sees the two lads standing beside him: 'Who are these?' he asks. They are my sons, Joseph answers patiently ...remember Dad, you were beginning to bless them ... Jacob collects himself and proceeds! 'God, before whom my fathers did walk, the God which shepherded me all my life long unto this day, the Angel which redeemed me from all evil, bless the lads' (48.15,16).

Jacob uses a three-fold invocation of God in his blessing: God of my fathers: God my Shepherd: God my Redeemer. Jacob had clearly had a real experience of God during his wanderings, but what makes his statement really remarkable is the fact that he is the first to refer to God as a Shepherd and a Redeemer. Of course others before him had known

God in these ways, but it is Jacob who actually uses these terms. Jacob, who was so wayward, so difficult, so self-willed and so neglectful of the things of God, had more reason than most to value God for these gracious characteristics. And how encouraging this is for us: if God was prepared to redeem and to shepherd Jacob, then surely there is mercy still reserved for me!

But what about the staff? The writer in Hebrews refers to Jacob worshipping, and undoubtedly it is Jacob expressing these qualities of God, as Shepherd and as Redeemer which he has in mind - but what has leaning upon his staff' got to do with it all?

Jacobs staff will have become very meaningful to him. It will have symbolised two things. Firstly, that he was a pilgrim. He had no settled abode in this life and as the writer to the Hebrews says of all the Patriarchs: 'They looked for a better country, that is, a heavenly, wherefore God is not ashamed to be called their God, for He has prepared for them a city' (Hebrews 11.13-16). Jacob was able to look back over his life and acknowledge the Shepherding of God '...all his life long': not just while he was in the ways of God, but even while he was wayward and rebellious, God had been caring and overseeing his life.

Secondly: Jacobs staff will have served to remind him of his encounter with God. As a younger man he had met God in a mysterious encounter at a crisis point in his life. In some mysterious way God had wrestled with him and Jacob had learnt the lesson of dependence upon God (Genesis 32.24-32). He had emerged from that experience crippled, but blessed and renamed: 'Isaac: a Prince with God'. Ever afterwards he had been physically disabled and had had to use a staff. His staff will therefore have come to symbolise God's dealings with him. And on his death-bed Jacob acknowledged God, above all else, as his Redeemer. God in mercy had forgiven him and brought him into an eternal relationship with Himself.

What will I be like on my death-bed? This may be a morbid thought, but we would all do well to heed the advice of Bunyan: 'If a man would live well let him fetch his last day to him and make it always his company-keeper'. (The Interpreter in Pilgrim's Progress). I am sure that on my death-bed I will regret very many things, but will I acknowledge the Shepherding and the Reedeming of God in my life? I will no doubt think of many lost opportunities, but will I have passed on to my children and to others the things I have learnt about God? And what will lie beyond? A man is a fool if he doesn't prepare beforehand for death - the only certainty in life!

25

JOSEPH'S MESSAGE OF HOPE

'He gave commandment concerning his bones.'
Hebrews 11.22 KJV

Jacob has given his final blessing to his sons. He has dwelt on his past experiences of God. He was the most pilgrim-like of all of all the Patriarchs, or Pilgrim-Fathers, and in his wanderings, he had learnt much of God. Despite his self-will and selfishness, he had come to a deep understanding of God. He had had an encounter with God and he had come to know God as His the One Who redeemed him from all evil. He now lay back in the bed and breathed his last (49.28-33).

Following the wishes of his father, Joseph sets out with the rest of the family, some Egyptian guards and others, and they take the body of Jacob to the family burial ground, a cave in Canaan which Abraham had bought and in which each of the Patriarchs and most of their wives had been buried. They make a long detour round the south of the Dead Sea, exactly as the children of Israel would do 400 years later, presumably because of hostile tribes.

On their return to Egypt an unworthy suspicion crossed the minds of the brothers of Joseph. What if, now that their father is dead, Joseph decides to take revenge on them for the terrible things they had done to him many years before. What if his forgiveness was a sham and he really hated them and would now get even with them (15). So they concoct a story (they were good at that!) and sent it to Joseph - they don't even have the courtesy to face him. They claim that before their father died he had told them to go to him and ask yet again for his forgiveness.

How little they knew Joseph. Their thinking was distorted by their own evil ways, and they expected that everyone else would behave as they did. They could not see that a man could forgive and forget, and so they were unable to enter into the freedom and confidence that true forgiveness gives. Of course, twenty years and more of selfish living, of deceit and of much fresh evil distorts a man's thinking, and the mind of such men will not be sorted out easily. No wonder Paul writes about having to 'crucify the flesh', making a comparison with the slow and painful death of crucifixion.

Of course when a man becomes a Christian the Holy Spirit of God indwells the heart and mind of that man as he submits to the Lordship of Christ, and as he absorbs more and more Scripture into his thinking, and works it out in daily living. And so the writer to the Hebrews encourages us: 'Therefore let us go on to maturity, not laying again the foundation of repentance'. (Hebrews 6.1)

That is: enter into the freedom that Christ gives, the freedom of a full and loving relationship within which God, by His Holy Spirit, helps us to become the best we can be in Him. And don't hamper the growth of that relationship by going over and over the past. After all, to do so implies a doubt of God, and a disbelief in His forgiveness.

The book of Genesis ends with the death of Joseph. As his father had done, Joseph left precise instructions about his burial. He was to lie in a coffin on Egypt, but when the children of Israel left Egypt, as God had promised they would, they were to take his remains with them back to Canaan, the land which God had given them (25).

Having been a most important official in Egypt, a prominent monument will probably have been built for the coffin. Just think of the encouragement and hope that that coffin will have brought to the children of Israel during their 400 years of exile, ending in slavery. They would look at the monument and tell each other: Remember, one day we are to take those bones away out of here to our own land ...remember, Joseph said, God will visit you and will bring you out of this land to the land which He gave to Abraham, and you will carry my bones with you (24,25).

The Godly life of Joseph and his dying instructions carried an enduring message of hope and confidence in God which was to sustain and encourage countless others. Perhaps this is why the writer to the Hebrews, in his 'thumb-nail' autobiography of Joseph says nothing of all his worldly success and prominence but simply: he made mention of the departing of the children of Israel, and gave commandment concerning his bones.

The symbol of hope Joseph left his family was his bones.

Jesus left us an empty tomb!

APPENDIX

The prayers of Jacob

I doubt if there is a man who never, never prays. In a crisis, in an emergency, what man doesn't say 'God help me!' Someone has said that the prayers of a man reveal what is deepest in his heart. He will at some time reveal by his prayers the people, or the things that he cares about most.

Several prayers of Jacob are recorded and they show what was in the heart of Jacob on each occasion. Consider just three of his prayers. They show an interesting development in the basic thinking of Jacob, and an enormous increase in his concept of God and his own relationship with God.

1. Jacob's prayer when a young man.

Jacob had caused so much trouble that he was virtually thrown out of his home! He had cheated his brother repeatedly. He had deceived his father Isaac. His mother Rebekah called him aside and warned him to get out quickly before his brother took vengeance and murdered him, but she told Isaac that she had sent their son to his uncle in the hope that he might find a cousin to marry (Genesis 27.41-46).

The first night out from home, Jacob lay down on the open field to sleep. He had a disturbed night. He dreamt, and in the morning, realising the predicament he was in, he was terrified. So he prayed:

> And Jacob vowed a vow, saying, If God will be with me,
> and will keep me in this way that I go, and will give me

bread to eat, and raiment to put on, so that I come again to my father's house in peace; then shall the LORD be my God...... and of all that thou shalt give me I will surely give the tenth unto thee. (Genesis 28.20-22) KJV

A strange prayer - and yet, fair is fair! It was a reasonable bargain. If God would keep his part, then Jacob would pay God back. Fair is fair!

Many men today pray this same kind of prayer - and after all, it seems fair and reasonable. I've done my part, now let God do his part. 'I've lived a good life, I've never hurt anyone - and I've even gone to church and put something in the bag on occasions. Now fair is fair - I've done my bit, so You do yours, God, and see I'm all right in the next world!'

But God doesn't bargain. God made us and he made the rules. And God cannot be paid off with a tenth, nor will he be paid off by a little bit of 'do gooding'! His demands are perfection - sinlessness. No less!

In any case, it looks as if Jacob forgot his wretched bargain. He went down to the home of Laban, his uncle, and there he started all the cheating and deceiving and lying again. Indeed things got so bad that he had to leave that home too in a hurry.

2. His prayer many years later.

A crisis arose. Jacob heard that the brother he had wronged so badly was coming to meet him with 400 armed men. Jacob was alone and defenceless. He knew the most likely outcome was death. And so he prayed.

Most men pray in a crisis. When they are at their wits end. When their resources have run out. So with Jacob. He prayed:

Lord, I am not worthy of the least of all
the mercies, and of all the truth,
which thou hast shewed unto thy servant' (Genesis 32.10) KJV

That night, Jacob had serious dealings with God. He cast himself on the mercy of God and he begged forgiveness. No bargaining now - just an appeal to God to save him. And that night Jacob was utterly changed. The events that followed showed just how different he was. God came into his life, and things were different!

It is only when a man stops parading his own works, stops thinking that he can do it his way ....and it is only when God comes into a life that there is a real change - the Bible later calls it 'new birth', 'a new creation'!

Nevertheless, the deception continued, despite his prayer! (Genesis 33.12-19) NIV

3. His last prayer.

Jacob is an old man. He is about to give his sons his last blessing. He makes a pathetic picture. He is disabled. He has difficulty standing up, and he has to support himself with a stick. He is almost blind and cannot distinguish one son from another. His memory has almost gone and he rambles as he talks. Genesis 48 gives a sad, but a very true and vivid picture of an old, old man. And very soon after this, Jacob did die.

And yet, Jacob prays with great assurance and confidence, and despite his feebleness and poor memory, the words of his prayer are very clear. He lifted his eyes to heaven and he prayed:

> God who has been my shepherd all my life to this day....
> who has delivered me from all evil (Genesis 48.15) NIV

Jacob looks back over a long and full life. He says nothing about himself. Nothing about the wasted years, the cheating, the lying and the deceit. Nor any mention of the bargain he had made with God as a young man. Rather, he focuses on God alone.....

You have shepherded me ...all the days of my life!
And you have redeemed me from all evil.

Professor Peter Elwood is medically qualified and for over 50 years he worked as an epidemiologist. For 21 years he led a research unit, and for 24 years following retirement he has held an honorary chair in the School of Medicine in Cardiff University.

Elwood's medical work has always been focused on prevention, rather than the treatment of disease, and one of his main concerns has been the evaluation of evidence. He has published over 500 research papers in scientific journals.

For a period of 14 years, Elwood led a Baptist Church in Pontypridd, South Wales, as a part-time lay pastor.

In 2012 Elwood was awarded OBE for 'Services to health'.